Higher Education Reconsidered

SUNY SERIES, CRITICAL ISSUES IN HIGHER EDUCATION
Jason E. Lane and D. Bruce Johnstone, editors

Also in this series

Universities and Colleges as Economic Drivers
edited by Jason E. Lane and D. Bruce Johnstone

Higher Education Systems 3.0
edited by Jason E. Lane and D. Bruce Johnstone

Building a Smarter University
edited by Jason E. Lane

Higher Education Reconsidered

EXECUTING CHANGE TO
DRIVE COLLECTIVE IMPACT

Edited by
Jason E. Lane

Foreword by
Nancy L. Zimpher

Published by State University of New York Press, Albany

© 2015 State University of New York

All rights reserved

Printed in the United States of America

No part of this book may be used or reproduced in any manner whatsoever without written permission. No part of this book may be stored in a retrieval system or transmitted in any form or by any means including electronic, electrostatic, magnetic tape, mechanical, photocopying, recording, or otherwise
without the prior permission in writing of the publisher.

For information, contact State University of New York Press, Albany, NY
www.sunypress.edu

Production, Ryan Morris
Marketing, Michael Campochiaro

Library of Congress Cataloging-in-Publication Data

Higher Education Reconsidered : Executing Change to Drive Collective Impact /
    edited by Jason E. Lane ; foreword by Nancy L. Zimpher
        pages cm. — (SUNY series, critical issues in higher education)
    Includes bibliographical references and index.
    ISBN 978-1-4384-5953-0 (hardcover : alk. paper)
    ISBN 978-1-4384-5952-3 (pbk. : alk. paper)
    ISBN 978-1-4384-5954-7 (e-book)
    1. Education, Higher—United States.   I. Lane, Jason E., editor of
compilation.
    2015946017

10   9   8   7   6   5   4   3   2   1

Contents

ILLUSTRATIONS

FOREWORD

Bringing Collective Impact to Higher Education

NANCY L. ZIMPHER

The United States has a long history of developing trailblazing education policies and practices to reach more people and enrich more lives. The belief in the value of education, that the health of any society depends on the education of its citizenry, is seminal to our identity and progress as a nation.

From the passage of the Morrill Land-Grant Act in 1862 and the GI Bill in 1944, to the founding of the National Science Foundation in 1950 and NASA in 1958 to the 1965 Higher Education Act and beyond, the United States has been, from early in its history, the world's leader in education and research innovation. The United States has continually pushed the boundaries of access and deepened the pool of humanity's knowledge of itself and the universe.

But over the last three decades, our global education rankings have fallen. The United States has not kept pace, and other developed nations have caught up and passed us. Our need to reclaim the position as first in the world in education is not for mere bragging rights—it is because our nation is an incomparable combination of vastness and diversity and principles. As such, we have the responsibility to our 320 million residents and to the world to ensure that every student leaves school prepared to really *live* in the world today—prepared to learn, to reason, to have productive and fulfilling careers, to be engaged citizens.

And so, the changing needs of our nation are calling on us to innovate again—to adapt and rethink our approach to education *as a whole*, from cradle to career, for every student in every zip code. This kind of sea change does not happen overnight, but it does need to happen quickly. And so we are pushing, together.

Therein lies the essence of this volume, which shares its title with the eye-opening, thought-provoking conference from which it emerged, *Higher Education Reconsidered: Executing Change to Drive Collective Impact.* Here we present to you a series of viewpoints on how institutions across society, not just colleges and universities, have employed different approaches to effect transformative, meaningful, and necessary change. Different sectors have a lot to learn from one other. It is time we start watching and listening. SUNY was thrilled to facilitate the conversation, drawing advice from the best and brightest in other fields, so that we may begin to apply their practices to meeting our goals.

How can institutions create meaningful collective impact and change? We placed this question on the table when we brought together more than 400 thought leaders from across sectors and across the nation. Further, we explored how we leave our individual agendas at the door in the name of working together toward achieving common goals. Clearly, these questions are big, and perhaps they are even bigger for higher education than any other sector because higher education has so long operated in its own, sometimes rarefied, silo, apart from the other education sectors.

President Barack Obama and Secretary of Education Arne Duncan have framed higher education's specific challenge around what they call an "iron triangle" (Duncan, 2009). That is to say, for colleges and universities to truly serve society, they must get three things right: affordability, accessibility, and accountability.

Toward that end, and to show how far we have to go to meet these goals, data show that the United States will not meet the completion rates set forth by the White House, the Lumina Foundation, and others at our current pace. Instead, goals for 2020 are projected to be met in 2037, goals for 2025 in 2054 (Kelly, 2010). This projected outcome is, clearly, not good enough. But higher education cannot fix this inadequate trajectory or meet its education goals on its own.

At SUNY we are building our efforts in this area around an idea at the core of the collective impact approach to improve the success of students, advance the lives of New York citizens, and strengthen the communities we serve. To do this we are identifying what works and putting our energy and resources toward doing more of it.

Of course, this is a simplified version of what needs to happen. How do we identify what works? What measurement systems do we use? What data are good? How do we convince everyone to pull together in one direction? And once we know what works, how do we fund it? How do we sustain the work? These questions represent just a few of those that need to be answered—and the answers need to be put into practice.

Here is where collective impact comes into play, and why we convened this conference. With all the competing interests, goals, priorities, and funding streams, what challenges can we in higher education tackle together? How can we use collective impact to truly drive the changes we need to see?

First, the key to creating collective impact is building a cross-sector partnership. We call this part of the process *building the table*: convening stakeholders from all constituent groups. In higher education, this strategy means enlisting thinkers and doers from both inside and outside the university's door. It means engaging K–12 partners, business and community leaders, elected officials, philanthropic organizations, and government agencies. Together, the individuals at the table must agree to formulate and commit to a shared vision and shared accountability.

Second, those at the table must select common, reliably measurable outcome indicators. You cannot change what you cannot measure.

Third, creating collective impact requires establishing cooperation and collaboration between organizations, departments, campuses, and systems to work on developing mutually reinforcing practices that drive the work forward.

Fourth, and finally, we must sustain what works. The long and short of it is that we must institutionalize the effective practices that move the dial. Too often we hear of a program that really worked—until the grant ran out, or the director moved on, or the institution decided to head in another direction. Real, sustainable change means changing the system itself.

Studying collective impact is itself a newly emerging field, but the practice of *creating* collective impact is as old as society. Really, it is what society *is*—human beings creating systems and solving problems together out of tried-and-tested practices. Doing more of what works and less of what does not. Striving toward continuous improvement. Working smarter to work better.

As the authors in this volume and our conference participants demonstrate, the collective impact approach to problem solving can, and I would argue, *must*, be used to address society's most pressing challenges. In the United States in 2015, that includes expanding education access, completion, and success.

At the State University of New York, the largest comprehensive university system in the nation, we are making it our business to lead the charge toward creating collective impact throughout the length of the education pipeline. We are making it our business to force a shift from a competitive or disinterested mindset between sectors to a collaborative, engaged one. We are making it our business to create a whole education sector, from prekindergarten to and through college, that rises to meet our nation's needs and creates a high quality of life for every student, every family, every community, one partnership at a time.

REFERENCES

Duncan, A. (2009). Rethinking higher education: Beyond the iron triangle. *Trusteeship* 12(5). Retrieved from http://agb.org/trusteeship/2009/septemberoctober/rethinking-higher-education-beyond-the-iron-triangle

Kelly, P. J. (2010). *Closing the college attainment gap between the U.S. and most educated countries, and the contributions to be made by the states*. Boulder, CO: National Center for Higher Education Management Systems.

ACKNOWLEDGMENTS

Nearly five years ago, SUNY set forth to develop a platform for discussing some of the most complex and important issues confronting higher education. The result was the SUNY Critical Issues in Higher Education conference (SUNYCON) and book series, which brings together thought leaders from across the world to address and debate how higher education is transforming and what responsibilities academic leaders have to respond to and lead such transformations. In 2011, we launched the series from Buffalo, New York, with a focus on the growing connection between higher education and economic development. The following year, we shifted the location to New York City and focused our attention on the evolution of state systems of higher education and the role they play in fostering a more collaborative enterprise focused on student success. In 2013, we set a foundation for how to build a "Smarter University" through the use of data, Big and small, to revolutionize student success efforts, research approaches, and academic programming.

A common theme among these topics was that the academy was in the midst of change. So, with SUNYCON 2014, we focused our attention on change. But not just change for the sake of change. Instead, we brought together leaders from government, industry, academia, and the social sector to dig deep into the idea of creating change in order to foster collective impact, that is, how we create collaborative enterprises that bring together multiple organizations to have a real impact on the most pressing issues facing humankind. Speakers at the conference examined efforts that worked to house the homeless, reduce unnecessary deaths in hospitals, and fix the leaks in the education pipeline. Their job was not just to inform us of *what* they did but *how* they created and sustained large-scale change. This volume is derived from those conversations and seeks to help readers grapple with the challenges of change and how to create opportunities for collective impact.

This volume and the associated conference are possible only because of the efforts of many individuals. As with any attempt to give thanks to specific individuals, someone will surely be omitted, for which I apologize in advance. For the second year, B. Alex Finsel provided research support and was a valued coauthor of the first chapter. As always, the careful eye of our copy editor Sarah Fuller Klyberg provided keen insight in the development of the manuscript. Johanna Kendrick-Holmes, Juliette Price, and Lauren McCabe were my compatriots in developing the conference and volume. We spent countless hours on the phone and in person developing the conference program and dealing with the logistics. As always, the support from the SUNY Press team has been outstanding and far beyond the call of duty—special thanks go to Beth Bouloukos, Donna Dixon, Fran Keneston, James Peltz, and Ryan Morris for shepherding the Critical Issues book series, bringing these volumes quickly to production, and promoting them broadly. Special thanks to all of the authors included in this volume. Their contributions shed light on the challenges of change and importance of collective impact. Finally, great appreciation goes to SUNY chancellor Nancy Zimpher for her vision in creating this series and recognizing the importance of supporting research and writing on public higher education.

And, special thanks go to my wife Kari and our daughter, Emerson, whose love, support, and encouragement make finishing a project like this both possible and much more fun.

Jason E. Lane
Albany, N.Y.

INTRODUCTION

JASON E. LANE

Higher education is often criticized as being slow to change, yet colleges and universities are among the only institutions, public or private, that have been able to endure for centuries. That endurance is in part linked to their ability to be both separate from and responsive to changing economic, political, and social demands. Higher education does change, but not always as rapidly as critics may like. What we teach, how we teach, and whom we teach continue to evolve. Over the last two centuries, we have layered research, service, and economic and community development upon the traditional teaching mission of the university.

One aspect, however, that has remained constant is the isolated nature of higher education, with colleges and universities competing with each other for students, faculty members, and resources. One consequence of this situation is that institutions have focused primarily on the micro-level issues on their specific campuses—a perspective that inhibits their ability to address the larger macro-level changes that are occurring.

Students now swirl through higher education. Data suggest that almost 40% of undergraduate students in the United States attend more than one higher education institution, with many of these students moving vertically and horizontally, even reversing from a four-year institution to a two-year institution (Shapiro, Dundar, Wakhungu, Yuan, & Harrell, 2015). Moreover, the conditions for successfully completing a college degree are set even before a student reaches college, starting from the early childhood years though high school and beyond (for nontraditional students). Therefore, as is discussed in chapter 1, focusing only on the experience of a student while he or she is at a particular institution does not address the macro-level issues that inhibit the opportunity of tens of thousands of students to complete a college degree. Multicampus systems of higher education have an opportunity, because of their coordinated governance structure, to develop models through which multiple campuses work together to help students move through the postsecondary educational pipeline and earn a credential; yet such efforts are only now beginning to gain traction across the United States.

One large-scale change initiative focused on improving student success is the National Association of System Heads' Taking Student Success to Scale (TS3) initiative to bring together the collective efforts of multicampus higher education systems in the United States to move the dial on completion. In 2014, leaders of many of the nation's largest collegiate systems gathered to identify three evidenced-based interventions that they believed, if implemented across their systems, would significantly increase the number of students completing a college credential. Those interventions were 1) revising pathways into college mathematics; 2) integrating predictive analytics into advising structures; and 3) implementing high-impact practices known to keep students in college. Each participating system agreed to adopt one or more of these strategies and committed staff to participate in a national learning community with representatives of other systems. At the time of this writing, more than 20 systems have committed to participating using their own resources and the national learning communities were just launching. While data are not yet available, the group is planning a national data collaborative to track impact. If successful, the collective impact of TS3 will increase the nation's completion productivity.

Moreover, successfully addressing the most significant challenges facing humankind (e.g., climate change, water shortages, declining natural resources, etc.) requires multi-institutional teams, sometimes spread across nations. Unfortunately, such collaborations are not prevalent. One example of such a broad collaboration is Europe's Large Hadron Collider. The collider was designed to uncover the building blocks of the universe and was built by a network of more than 10,000 scientists and engineers from hundreds of universities and labs around the world (Highfield, 2008). In this case, the European Organization for Nuclear Research (CERN) served as the backbone of the enterprise through which all partners' activities were planned, coordinated, and funded (see chapter 1 for a discussion of backbone organizations). Such examples of large-scale collaboration remain rare, with governments and other funders too often reinforcing more isolated efforts by creating structures that reward institutions for having the single best idea and incentivize the isolation of the impact of institutions' efforts from all other activities.

Finally, there is increasing recognition of colleges' and universities' critical role as anchors within their communities, which is accompanied by rising expectations that they will become the engines of economic and social revitalization. They cannot play this role in isolation, however. To realize genuine impact on economic and social issues, colleges and universities must work collaboratively with different stakeholders within their communities. Take, for example, the low high school graduation rates that persist in many communities across the United States. Too often, higher education leaders are not present at the table when communities are seeking to address this challenge. Yet colleges and universities educate the teachers who teach in the local school districts and enroll the students who graduate from local high schools. Higher education institutions are very much part of the social and economic ecosystem and need to work with others in the community to address graduation and other K–12 education issues. Successful examples of higher education's engagement in the broader social sector are discussed in chapters 4 and 5. In a growing number of communities across the United States, higher education institutions are working with dozens of local stakeholders to collaboratively improve the educational experience of those in the K–12 educational pipeline. Yet, only a handful of these efforts to foster large-scale change have been successful. Why?

While collaboration is typically a rallying cry for change, often few results are actually realized via collaborative processes. It is easy to gather to discuss change and then expect others to do the work that will accomplish the desired outcomes, but collaboration to identify needed changes must be followed by collaboration to implement those changes. This volume focuses on this very issue: What is the science behind large-scale change? While there can be multiple ways to effect change, the strategy that has been labeled *collective impact* (CI) has proven to be successful in large-scale change efforts as diverse as improving high school graduation rates, cleaning polluted water sources, and tackling childhood obesity.

In this volume, contributors discuss changing one's mindset from that of isolated organization-specific results to one of collective impact—sharing data, ideas, and processes that work so that they might be applied in as many contexts as possible. Economist John Maynard Keynes (1935) once said, "The difficulty lies not in the new ideas, but in escaping from the old ones" (p. 5). In the case of higher education, the challenge is not to recognize the value of acting collectively but to be willing to set aside the expectations of acting in isolation.

The intention of this volume is to confront the notion of isolated impact, unpack some of the challenges associated with change, and provide readers with the tools that are necessary to engage in collective impact. In the first chapter, Jason Lane, B. Alex Finsel, and Taya Owens, from the State University of New York, provide an introduction to collective impact, illustrating the need to move from competition to collaboration to impact. Beyond recognizing the need to shift the way in which people view the world, leaders will need to facilitate a shift in the way in which their organizations work. In the second chapter, Scott Keller and Carolyn Aiken, both of McKinsey & Company, critically examine many of the myths associated with change management and provide readers with insights about how to manage change in their own organizations.

In chapter 3, Jonathan Gagliardi, deputy director of the National Association of System Heads, explores in more depth the tendency of higher education institutions to operate in isolation. He argues that higher education systems provide a natural foundation for addressing many of the macro-level challenges now confronting them.

Chapter 4, co-authored by Jeff Edmondson, managing director of Strive, and Nancy Zimpher, former chancellor of the University of Cincinnati, explains how they created the Strive Partnership using a process that would come to be labeled "collective impact." This effort focused on plugging the holes in the cradle-to-career pipeline in Cincinnati by pulling together multiple community part-ners, creating a shared vision, and aligning their collective efforts and resources toward achieving mutually agreed upon goals. The Strive Partnership has often been held up as an exemplar of the collective impact model; but Edmondson and Zimpher also push against what they call the "sanitized" version portrayed in various write-ups and explain the daily struggles associated with this work.

In chapter 5, David Weerts, director of the Jandris Center for Innovative Higher Education; Chris Rasmussen, vice president of the Association of Governing Boards; and Virajita Singh, a senior research fellow with the College of Design and assistant vice pro-vost for equity and diversity at the University of Minnesota, explain how they have borrowed lessons from design thinking to implement collective impact strategies. They share lessons learned from the Higher Education Redesign Initiative, a Minnesota-based project that has engaged multiple partners across sectors to create new models of educational delivery to improve the success of diverse learners.

Juliette Price, interim director of Albany Promise, provides in chapter 6 a case study of how the community in Albany, New York, used the collective impact model to replicate the Strive model by laying out how the model needed to be adapted for that context. Given that the focus of this volume is on higher education, Price pays special attention to the role that local higher education lead-ers and institutions played in supporting the development of the network.

The seventh and final chapter is extracted from a panel discus-sion at the fourth annual SUNY Critical Issues in Higher Education conference that was moderated by David Leonhardt of the *New York Times*. The panelists were Jeff Edmondson (StriveTogether), Jason Helgerson (New York State Department of Health), Danette Howard (Lumina Foundation), James Kvaal (White House), Becky Margiotta (100,000 Homes Campaign), and Joe McCannon (100,000 Lives Campaign). Each panelist has in-depth experience with large-scale change, and through their discussion they bring to life the challenges and opportunities associated with collective impact.

Higher education is an enduring part of the social fabric of the United States and beyond. Many challenges lie ahead, and some of them are quite daunting. But if we can shift our way of thinking from isolated interests to collaborative goals and ultimately to collective impact, we can change the world.

REFERENCES

Highfield, R. (2008, September 16). Large Hadron Collider: Thirteen ways to change the world. *Daily Telegraph*. Retrieved from http://www.telegraph.co.uk/news/science/large-hadron-collider/3351899/Large-Hadron-Collider-thirteen-ways-to-change-the-world.html

Keynes, J. M. (1935). *The general theory of employment, interest, and money*. New York, NY: Harcourt, Brace.

Shapiro, D., Dundar, A., Wakhungu, P. K., Yuan, X., & Harrell, A. (2015, July). *Transfer and mobility: A national view of student movement in postsecondary institutions, fall 2008 cohort* (Signature Report No. 9). Herndon, VA: National Student Clearinghouse Research Center.

1

COLLECTIVE LEADERSHIP IN HIGHER EDUCATION

Moving from Competition to Collaboration to Impact

JASON E. LANE, B. ALEX FINSEL, AND TAYA OWENS

ABSTRACT

Higher education has been structured around the concept of isolated impact at individual institutions. This chapter argues that to address some of the most significant challenges facing higher education and society at large, a more collective response is needed. The authors unpack the basic concepts associated with collective impact and collective leadership.

The calls for higher education to change seem to intensify with every media cycle. Some are calling for higher education to expand access, increase completion, and lower costs. Others expect colleges and universities to be economic and community saviors, ranging from serving as anchor institutions within communities to producing the next great innovation that will drive the national knowledge economy. In many ways, such calls for change are not so much about changing higher education, per se, but about leveraging the resources of higher education to meet some of the nation's and the world's most pressing social and economic issues.

In part, the confusion about how to respond to calls for change in higher education is due to the nature of the concerns that are being addressed and how the existing system seeks to address them. First, expanding access, increasing completion, driving economic development, and ensuring that students are college and career ready are not merely technical issues that can be quickly resolved; they are adaptive problems that necessitate complex solutions and the engagement of multiple stakeholders. Technical problems can be addressed with direct responses, such as when one's computer breaks. However, adaptive challenges can be difficult to identify; require a mind shift in one's values, beliefs, or approaches to work; engage people confronting the challenge in the work of solving the problem; and require collaboration among multiple stakeholders (Heifetz & Laurie, 1997; Heifetz & Linsky, 2002).

Second, higher education and the larger nonprofit sector tend to operate in what Kania and Kramer (2011) call "isolated impact." Higher education is by design a decentralized enterprise, wherein colleges and universities tend to operate in isolation from, if not outright competition with, each other. Yet if we look to our colleagues in K–12 education, healthcare, and the social sector, collaborative initiatives are moving the dial on big, messy, and important goals. A community network in Cincinnati, called the Strive Partnership, significantly improved high school graduation rates as well as the number of preschool children prepared for kindergarten across three large schools districts (see chapter 4). The 100,000 Lives Campaign, through the Institute for Healthcare Improvements, has brought together hospitals to collectively reduce morbidity and mortality rates in U.S. hospitals (see chapter 7). Shape Up Somerville, a citywide effort to reduce obesity in elementary school children, resulted in a statistically significant decrease in the body mass index of the Massachusetts community's children between 2002 and 2005 (Kania & Kramer, 2011).[1]

Why have these efforts been so effective? They recognized that the issues that they were addressing were adaptive in nature, and they followed a collective impact (CI) approach to executing change: creating a shared agenda among multiple partners, defining an agreed-upon set of metrics to measure success, implementing a set of mutually reinforcing activities, focusing on continuous improvement, and creating an organizational backbone to support the collaboration. Essentially, varied stakeholders with a bold vision decided to work together to achieve a shared vision by using data and scaling up evidence-based interventions. They sought to have a collective impact on a major social issue.

This volume explores the concept of collective impact and examines how higher education institutions might use such an approach to address their most complex challenges. Contributors to the volume explore how higher education institutions can contribute to confronting major social challenges and how they can work together to scale change beyond a single institution. However, the approach of this book is not to suggest that collective impact is a way in which to "save" higher education. Rather, the authors in this volume understand that higher education has an important role to play in addressing major social and economic challenges. Collective impact is focused on creating change to drive real impact in the communities, big and small, in which we live.

This volume is about how to respond to adaptive challenges and achieve collective impact. Readers will find examples and instructions to help them execute change in order to drive collective impact. Understanding how other sectors, such as health care, business, and the social sector, tackled their adaptive challenges can inform us about what collective impact looks like and how to get there. Readers are invited to consider how they, their institutions, and their communities might benefit from such an approach.

HIGHER EDUCATION RECONSIDERED: SHIFTING FROM ISOLATED RESULTS TO COLLECTIVE IMPACT

Change does not come easy. In fact, 20 years ago Kotter (1995) reported that only 30% of change efforts were successful. It is doubtful that this proportion has increased markedly since then. In chapter 2, Keller and Aiken lay out many of the inconvenient truths associated with popular change efforts—truths that, unless confronted, can lead to failed attempts at change. In thinking about fostering a collective impact mindset in higher education, one of the most significant inconvenient truths is that, as a sector, higher education is designed to be competitive, not collaborative, and focused on isolated results, not collective impacts. In order to move higher education toward a collective approach to addressing problems, we need to realize that our existing structures struggle against such an approach.

The title of this book is partly borrowed from Ernie Boyer's (1990) influential book *Scholarship Reconsidered: Priorities of the Professoriate*, in which he argued that academia should reconsider how its views of research and scholarship "define the work of faculty in ways that reflect more realistically the full range of academic and civic mandates" (p. 16). His concern was that scholarship was being too narrowly defined, squeezing out important faculty contributions such as translational research and the scholarship of teaching and learning (as opposed to the scholarship of discovery, which had come to dominate the view of many tenure committees). While not addressed directly in this book except for a brief mention in chapter 7, Boyer's comments have relevance to this discussion in that rewarding faculty members for engaging in the community and using their scholarship to benefit community initiatives, such as those that use a collective impact approach, can go a long way to incentivize meaningful involvement of faculty members in social innovations.

> **In thinking about fostering a collective impact mindset in higher education, one of the most significant inconvenient truths is that, as a sector, higher education is designed to be competitive, not collaborative, and focused on isolated results, not collective impacts.**

By using the term "reconsidered," the desire is to encourage readers to reconsider the isolated ways in which higher education functions and consider moving toward a more collective approach to achieving impact. It is not just that higher education may choose to operate in silos, however. External entities reinforce this approach. As Kania and Kramer note:

> Most funders, faced with the task of choosing a few grantees from many applicants, try to ascertain which organizations make the greatest contribution toward solving a social

problem. Grantees, in turn, compete to be chosen by emphasizing how their individual activities produce the greatest
effect. Each organization is judged on its own potential to
achieve impact, independent of the numerous other organizations that may also influence the issue. And when a
grantee is asked to evaluate the impact of its work, every
attempt is made to isolate that grantee's individual influence
from all other variables. (2011, para. 11)

Take for example the so-called Completion Agenda, a broad-based
effort by policy makers and foundations to significantly improve
the number of students who graduate from U.S. colleges and universities. This call was precipitated by growing recognition of the
important intersection between educational attainment and economic prosperity and was compounded by data that suggested that
the United States had moved from being the most-well-educated
country in the world to being the 10th most well educated.[2]

It is easy to see the lack of shared vision within higher education
by examining the goals that the federal government and two major
foundations have expressed for it. President Barack Obama in his
joint address to Congress in 2009 declared that, by 2020, the United States will regain its position as having the highest proportion
of college graduates in the world. The Lumina Foundation (2015)
has committed to increasing the proportion of "Americans with
high-quality degrees, certificates and other credentials to 60 percent
by 2025" (para. 1). Meanwhile, the Gates Foundation (2015) has
a goal of ensuring that "all students who seek the opportunity are
able to complete a high-quality, affordable postsecondary education
that leads to a sustaining career" (para. 1). Each of these statements
points to the noble goal of increasing the number of students who
complete college, but there is a lack of shared understanding of
timing, intent, and even definition of credentials.

The story becomes even more problematic when we consider
the actual results of these efforts. Policy makers, foundations, and
educational leaders have led varied attempts to increase the number
of students who complete college, and as a result, one is likely
to see some changes at individual campuses and within specific
programs, but no significant changes at scale have occurred. The
combined impact of these efforts has been marginal, barely moving

the needle. For the United States to be on par with the most-well-educated nations in the world by 2025 (five years after the president's goal), the nation's colleges and universities would need to produce approximately 64 million more degree earners since 2005. However, data suggest that we are on track to only produce 48 million, leaving a gap of 16 million degrees (Kelly, 2010).

The challenges have too often been thought of as technical problems rather than adaptive challenges, and they have been addressed in isolation rather than through a collective impact lens.

Similar stories can be told about increasing access, overcoming racial disparities, reducing the need for remediation, improving learning outcomes, and so forth. There are many stories of successful changes at a specific institution or on an individual campus, but problems still persist at the national level. In part, this gap exists because efforts have been scattered, not coordinated, and few leaders have demonstrated the ability to create real, sustainable change in higher education. The challenges have too often been thought of as technical problems rather than adaptive challenges, and they have been addressed in isolation rather than through a collective impact lens.

UNDERSTANDING COLLECTIVE IMPACT

Not all problems can be solved in the same way. Accordingly, organizations need to know the difference between adaptive and technical problems. Technical problems are well defined with known solutions, and a few organizations are capable of implementing these solutions. In contrast, adaptive problems are more complex since a clear solution does not exist, and if a solution does exist, no single organization has the authority or capacity to enact change. To address adaptive problems, organizations need to abandon individual agendas and work with other organizations across sectors toward shared goals. Collaboration is a step in this process, but it is insufficient. Unlike collaboration, collective impact is the process of bringing together a committed "group of important actors from different sectors to a common agenda for solving a specific social problem" (Kania & Kramer, 2011). Moreover, successful collective impact initiatives must balance decentralized ownership of the initiative with the need to have "a centralized infrastructure, a dedicated staff, and a structured process that leads to a common agenda, shared measurement, continuous communication, and mutually reinforcing activities among all participants" (Kania & Kramer, 2011, para. 6).

The problems facing higher education today are adaptive in nature and thus require a different, multifaceted approach to solve them in a meaningful and significant manner: collective impact. In a groundbreaking article, Kania and Kramer (2011) identified five necessary components for successful implementation of collective impact initiatives that cut across collective impact strategies in multiple social sectors. We should note that a common criticism of this work is that it is not possible to boil down complex change initiatives to a simple set of characteristics (see chapter 7), as there is no way to predict what exactly will be needed to pull together and sustain a diverse community of stakeholders. Moreover, such lists do not capture the amount of sweat equity that is required to keep such collaborative efforts moving forward and to insure that individual actors contribute to the betterment of the whole. With that caveat, the following five components are a useful way to begin to understand the type of structure needed to start and sustain a collective impact initiative.

Common agenda. The first priority for establishing a collective impact strategy is the identification of a shared goal or goals and a common understanding of where the participants will focus their efforts in order to achieve the goal. It is nearly impossible to achieve significant impact when there is a lack of shared understanding and no common agenda. In such a context, it is not surprising that there is very limited progress on achieving any of an initiative's goals.

The expectation of a common agenda does not mean that there has to be consensus on all details. Instead, Kania and Kramer (2011) explain, "Collective Impact requires that these differences be discussed and resolved" (para. 18). Ultimately, all participants must agree on the primary goal for the effort.

Shared measurement system. Having a shared goal means little if there is not a shared understanding of how success will be measured. The only way to determine if progress toward the goal is occurring is for partners to agree to common data definitions, regular collection of data, and use of data to drive decision making at both the collective and individual levels. Shared measurement insures that the actions of actors remain aligned and provides opportunity for shared accountability.

As mentioned in the previous section, there is a lack of understanding of the ultimate goal of the Completion Agenda. Since there is no agreement on what represents "completion" (e.g., degree, certificate, badge, etc.), it is not possible to determine shared measurements of success. Without such shared data, it is not possible to hold the myriad stakeholders accountable for their contributions, or lack of contributions, to achieving this goal.

Mutually reinforcing activities. A strength of the collective impact approach is that it does not require each participant to do the same thing. Rather, partners pursue coordinated activities within their domains of influence that can contribute to the overall goal. As Kania and Kramer (2011) explain, "The multiple causes of social problems, and the components of their solutions, are interdependent. They cannot be addressed by uncoordinated actions among isolated organizations" (para. 23).

To effect meaningful change, strategies to address most major social issues are typically implemented in stages. As discussed in chapter 4, the StriveTogether effort in Cincinnati focuses on expanding early childhood education and improving third grade reading levels as means for improving high school graduation rates. By focusing on these sublevel goals, improvement is more visible, whereas it may take years to see significant change in the high school graduation rate. Collective impact has been successful because partners have been able to pursue their own initiatives in ways that have contributed to the overall goal.

Continuous communication. Creating a shared vision, fostering trust, and holding each other accountable requires an incredible amount of communication. This communication needs to be regular and ongoing. Building a collective impact partnership also requires a great deal of time as actors need to let go of some of their own agendas and reshape their efforts to pursue the agreed-upon strategy. Participants "need time to see that their own interests will be treated fairly, and that decisions will be made on the basis of objective evidence and the best possible solution to the problem, not to favor the priorities of one organization over another" (Kania & Kramer, 2011, para. 27).

Backbone organization. A separate organization and staff are required to propel a network that is designed to foster collective impact, to serve as the network's backbone. Expecting organizations that are already overextended and their already overworked staffs, all of which are concerned with multiple initiatives that are competing for scarce resources, to provide support for the collective impact network often leads to failure. Kania and Kramer (2011) found that each of the collective impact initiatives that they studied developed a separate organization with the explicit purpose of facilitating collaboration and driving the efforts to achieve the participants' common agenda.

StriveTogether is an excellent example of a collective impact initiative that thrived through the Great Recession and expanded in its wake. The initiative is not a new program but a carefully structured, collaborative process that has brought the entire educational community together to work toward a common set of goals with shared measurement. The organization has over 300 leaders, including heads of influential private and corporate foundations, city government officials, heads of local organizations, presidents of eight universities and community colleges, and executive directors of 100 education-related nonprofit and advocacy groups. These 300 leaders created a common agenda to improve high school graduation rates, developed a shared set of metrics to track progress, enabled partners to focus efforts at multiple levels of the educational pipeline, met frequently to discuss progress, and developed a separate non-profit organization to serve as the backbone (see Edmondson, 2013) of the initiative. Most importantly, the partnership did not seek to create new interventions. Rather, it worked to identify those efforts that worked already and then focused on scaling those efforts up.

Cross-sector coordination is better suited to large-scale change than is the isolated impact of individual organizations. It is a new approach to change and requires a break from the traditional emphasis on independent action, which requires organizations to compete for funding. Collective impact is not a simple program, but it is a process and a new way of tackling complicated social problems. Valuing a singular contribution ignores the idea that complex problems have many variables.

SOCIAL PROBLEMS, HIGHER EDUCATION, AND COLLECTIVE IMPACT

Through their concurrent missions of teaching, research, and service as well as the increasing expectation to engage in economic and community development, institutions of higher education are connected to a wide array of social issues. As such, attempts to address such social issues through collective impact often necessitate the engagement of colleges and universities. Without their involvement, the desired change is likely to not be realized. As stated in the beginning of this chapter, there are many calls for reform in higher education to increase the number of individuals completing college. Much research supports the individual and societal benefits of increased completion. For example, increased education can contribute to increased monetary benefits and nonmonetary benefits to individuals, their families, and their communities at large (Carnevale & Rose, 2012; Wolfe & Haveman, 2001). Some of the benefits include: increased wages, increased income equality, increased health status, increased civic participation, increased social cohesion, reduced criminal activity, and reduced dependence on welfare transfers (or income-based entitlement programs).

These benefits do not exist in isolation. In other words, a linear relationship does not exist between educational attainment and social benefits. To address the many challenges confronting society, the actions of colleges and universities should be taken into consideration alongside other public service policies and in collaboration with a broad array of stakeholders. Several educational policy issues remain salient in the discussion of broader social welfare: access to early childhood education, access to equitable compulsory education, affordable postsecondary education, and training opportunities for shifting adult labor markets. In addition to the cognitive and health benefits of early childhood education (Isaacs & Roessel, 2008), research has shown that public investments into childcare subsidies have a positive effect on working-class families, especially single mothers (Herbst, 2010). Taking a look at the relationship in another way, a lack of early childhood education can have a negative impact on the local economy, both in terms of the high proportion of family income that is spent on childcare instead of elsewhere, as well as in terms of the limits of worker productivity due to insufficient care (Laughlin, 2013). The link to higher education is that colleges and universities are important anchor institutions in the communities in which they operate and house an array of resources that can be helpful in addressing many of the most important social issues facing humankind. Higher education institutions usually train the individuals who teach in the early childhood education setting, and the students who benefit from early childhood education will bring those benefits with them to colleges and universities years later.

Challenges such as expanding access, increasing degree completion, and driving economic growth require more than simply pulling a policy lever. They require systematic and collaborative arrangements that seek adaptive changes to alter the very ways in which we approach the work we do.

The collective impact approach is based on the belief that macro-outcomes of social issues are not the result of a linear production function. Rather they are the result of many micro-level decisions and actions that are made according to discrete rules. Processes also bring lagged effects to the forefront; interactions between actors at the local level are not immediately observable in system-level effects. Collective impact seeks to balance both actor processes (short-term behavior) and system effects (long-term impacts).

Challenges such as expanding access, increasing degree completion, and driving economic growth require more than simply pulling a policy lever. They require systematic and collaborative arrangements that seek adaptive changes to alter the very ways in which we approach the work we do.

UNIVERSITY AS BACKBONE AND/OR CONVENER

Colleges and universities may be one of the largest participants in a collective impact network. As such, they may be expected to take a leadership role in what Edmondson (2013) has described as the backbone or the convener. As described earlier, the backbone serves as the single primary entity responsible for coordinating the development of the civic infrastructure to support the initiative. The role of the backbone is differentiated from the role of conveners, who are responsible for working with relevant partners to drive forward outcomes in a section of the continuum of the problem that a collective impact network is addressing. While there should be only one backbone, there can be multiple conveners.

The backbone is critical for the success of the network. It fulfills four primary roles (Edmonson, 2013).

1. *Connect and support leaders.* A key role of the backbone is to make sure that all parties remain focused on the shared vision, and that their actions work to advance that vision. This responsibility often requires representatives of the backbone to meet with participants to discuss issues and concerns and ensure that the participants feel supported by the network.

2. *Establish the data management infrastructure.* The backbone is responsible for managing the data infrastructure; ensuring that there are shared definitions of data; and working with partners to collect, manage, and report data.

3. *Advocate for technical support.* The development of action plans to achieve the shared vision can be complicated when participants have difficulty accessing data, making connections with key players, or communicating about their work. The backbone can provide support, such as meeting facilitation, or help broker solutions to overcome other barriers.

4. *Marshall investments.* Many participants in the collective impact network spend a considerable amount of time fundraising to support their efforts. The backbone can play a critical role in working with private and public funders to support a comprehensive approach through the collective impact network and providing

funding to partners for clearly defined purposes. This role can actually free up partners' time so that they can focus on their core activities, rather than on fundraising.

The backbone organization may also serve in the role of convener. Conveners tend to play a more visible role than the backbone organization. They can convene the entire collective impact network or key subsets of the network whose participants are focused on the same goals. According to Edmondson (2013), the conveners have three primary responsibilities. First, they must engage participants in the work of the collaborative, overcoming concerns about additional workload that arise early on and ensuring that their work is driven by data. Second, they commit to facilitating the broader multisector network to ensure that participants work together and collectively move toward agreed-upon goals. Third, they ensure that action plans are continually updated so that the network achieves intermediate goals and continues to move toward achieving the shared vision.

Important for both the backbone and the convener is that they are unbiased toward any of the participants in the network. If participants perceive that bias exists, it can be difficult to foster trust and can significantly undermine the network's efforts.

MOVING TOWARD COLLECTIVE LEADERSHIP

The decentralized nature of higher education has led to a perception of colleges and universities as unitary actors, competing with each other for resources, students, and faculty members. This view has also led colleges and universities to practice a diffused approach when addressing national and regional challenges, such as the Completion Agenda described earlier. As a result, individual institutions may find ways to address challenges, but they lack the ability to effect broader environmental forces that reinforce the status quo, and they cannot scale initiatives to a level that can have significant impact. However, we need to be able to think beyond what happens solely within a given institution. We need to consider the larger environment in which higher education exists and how colleges and universities interact with each other and institutions in other sectors.

To address many of the challenges being laid before it, the higher education sector needs not just a collective impact approach. It also needs leaders who understand what is possible by fostering greater collaboration among colleges, universities, and other organizations. Opportunities for collective impact are plentiful, yet few take advantage of such opportunities. This lack of response is, in part, due to a lack of leadership. Advancing a collective impact strategy requires at least one person with the ability to see the situation in its entirety (as opposed to focusing only on his or her sphere of influence), accepting that others have knowledge needed to effect change, and a willingness to set aside his or her organization's agenda to develop and pursue a shared vision established by multiple stakeholders. Such individuals tend to be a catalyst for the development of a collective impact network because they understand that the collective action of the whole is the only way to achieve real impact on certain major social issues.

Higher education is facing challenges for which more collective impact leaders are needed. Such leaders can be difficult to identify and their characteristics mystifying. In their study of nonprofit organizations, Senge, Hamilton, and Kania (2015) studied several individuals that they believed to be collective leaders and identified three primary characteristics of collective leaders:

1. *Seeing the larger system.* Few people have the ability to fully understand the systemic nature of conditions that contribute to large social issues. Leaders tend to focus on problems that fall within their domain, often ignoring or deemphasizing the parts of the system that are beyond their control. The reality is that complex social issues require interventions at multiple levels. For example, most students now swirl through higher education, attending at least two institutions before they complete their degree (if they complete at all). Most campus presidents, however, see the student experience only during the time when the student is enrolled on their campus. Efforts to help students complete their degree at that campus fail to account for the way in which students now experience higher education. To really have an impact on the Completion Agenda, leaders who can understand the entirety of the student

experience, and see their piece as only one of several pieces in the puzzle, are needed. Rather than focusing solely on the student experience at one campus, higher education leaders at multiple institutions need to work together to develop supports that help students move more seamlessly through their multi-campus collegiate experience.

2. *Fostering reflection and generative conversations.* System leaders provide opportunities for groups to reflect on the way they do things, "holding up the mirror to see the taken-for-granted assumptions we carry into any conversation and appreciating how our mental models may limit us" (Senge et al., 2015, para. 11). To address adaptive problems, groups need to critically assess their assumptions, listening to other perspectives and working to shift their own perceptions of reality. This practice often requires recognition that individuals may perceive reality differently, as well as willingness to accept the existence of multiple realities.

3. *Moving from reactive problem solving to co-creating the future.* Change usually starts during times of distress, leading people to react to immediate problems rather than looking at underlying issues. System leaders help people move beyond reacting to problems, enabling them to find a way to build new visions for the future instead. Leaders enable people to understand their deeper aspirations and to create a collective confidence built on shared struggles and triumphs. "This shift involves not just building inspiring visions but facing difficult truths about the present reality and learning how to use the tension between vision and reality to inspire truly new approaches" (Senge et al., 2014, para. 12).

COLLECTIVE IMPACT IN HIGHER EDUCATION MOVING FORWARD

Many of the issues that are currently confronting higher education cannot be resolved using the same old approaches of isolated results—allowing institutions to find solutions that work on their campus, without considering either the long educational pipeline or the need to scale efforts to facilitate large-scale impact. External observers and stakeholders expect colleges and universities to transform the postsecondary educational experience, but the challenges are not technical in nature. Adaptive solutions are needed to confront the messy, complex, and multifaceted nature of the educational experience. Multiple stakeholders must be brought together to identify what works, implement what works, and track progress. One approach, and the one that is the focus of this book, is collective impact.

Just imagine if a collective impact approach were brought to the Completion Agenda. Rather than having each individual institution identify, via trial and error, strategies that work to improve completion on their campus, would it be possible to create a network of institutions that are dedicated to making progress on key areas that are known to have positive impacts on a student's ability to complete? Could we create a shared vision and common data metrics? Would it be possible to work with funders to support a common strategy that transcends multiple institutions—all working on similar strategies? What if we focused on scaling up proven interventions, rather than funding new efforts?

Bringing this hypothetical into reality is exactly what the National Association of System Heads (NASH) is attempting to do with their Taking Student Success to Scale (TS3) initiative. Recognizing that multi-campus systems of higher education have a built-in structure to facilitate a collaborative approach, NASH is working to create a collective impact network of systems (essentially a network of networks) to move the dial on completion. They have a shared vision of increasing the number of annual completions in the United States by 350,000 between 2014 and 2020. They have identified three strategies that are proven to have a positive impact on student completion rates (improving math pathway courses, using data analytics to guide course selection, and implementing high-impact practices). Subgroups of systems are working to identify short-term goals for each initiative. NASH serves as the backbone, coordinating the network, working with partners, and developing a data hub. The effort is just beginning, and results are not yet available, but we include the example here to illustrate what a collective impact effort may look like in higher education.

The real message of this book is that large-scale change is possible. Collective impact is not the only way to go about this work, but it is a model that can be used, adapted, and studied. What is important is that as a sector, higher education recognizes that efforts to pursue isolated results may help address certain technical problems, but a collective approach is needed to address the adaptive problems that it is currently confronting.

NOTES

1. More information about these and other collective impact efforts can be found in Kania and Kramer (2011).
2. This statement is based on the proportion of young people (25–34 years of age) with a college degree (associate's or higher), as reported annually by the Organisation for Economic Co-operation and Development (OECD, 2014).

REFERENCES

Boyer, E. (1990). *Scholarship reconsidered: Priorities of the professoriate*. San Francisco: Carnegie Foundation for the Advancement of Teaching.

Carnevale, A. P., & Rose, S. J. (2012). The convergence of postsecondary education and the labor market. In J. E. Lane & D. B. Johnstone (Eds.), *Universities and colleges as economic drivers* (pp. 163–190). Albany: State University of New York Press.

Edmondson, J. (2013, May 17). The difference between backbones and conveners in Collective Impact. Retrieved July 7, 2015 from http://www.strivetogether.org/blog/2013/05/the-difference-between-backbones-and-conveners-in-collective-impact/

Gates Foundation. (2015). Postsecondary success: Strategic overview. Retrieved July 28, 2015 from http://www.gatesfoundation.org/What-We-Do/US-Program/Postsecondary-Success

Heifetz, R. A., & Laurie, D. L. (1997). The work of leadership. *Harvard Business Review 75*(1), 124–134.

Heifetz, R. A., & Linsky, M. (2002). *Leadership on the line: Staying alive through the dangers of leading*. Boston, MA: Harvard Business School Press.

Heller, D. E. (1997). Student price response in higher education: An update to Leslie and Brinkman. *Journal of Higher Education 68*, 624–659. doi:10.2307/2959966

Herbst, C. M. (2010). The labor supply effects of child care costs and wages in the presence of subsidies and the earned income tax credit. *Review of Economics of the Household 8*, 199–230. doi:10.1007/s11150-009-9078-1

Isaacs, J. B., & Roessel, E. (2008). *Impacts of early childhood programs*. Retrieved from Brookings Institution website: http://www.brookings.edu/research/papers/2008/09/early-programs-isaacs

Kania, J., & Kramer, M. (2011, winter). Collective impact. *Stanford Social Innovation Review*. Retrieved from http://www.ssireview.org/articles/entry/collective_impact

Kelly, P. J. (2010). *Closing the college attainment gap between the U.S. and most educated countries, and the contributions to be made by the states*. Boulder, CO: National Center for Higher Education Management Systems.

Kotter, J. (1995, March–April). Leading change: Why transformation efforts fail. *Harvard Business Review 59*–67.

Laughlin, L. (2013). *Who's minding the kids? Child care arrangements: Spring 2011* (Report No. P70-135). Retrieved from U.S. Census Bureau website: https://www.census.gov/prod/2013pubs/p70-135.pdf

Lumina Foundation. (2015). *A stronger nation through higher education*. Indianapolis, IN.

Organisation for Economic Co-operation and Development (OECD). (2014). *Education at a Glance 2014: OECD Indicators*. Retrieved May 15, 2015 from http://www.oecd.org/education/eag.htm

Senge, P., Hamilton, H., & Kania, J. (2015, winter). The Dawn of System Leadership. *Stanford Social Innovation Review*. Retrieved from http://www.ssireview.org/articles/entry/the_dawn_of_system_leadership.

Wolfe, B., & Haveman, R. (2001). Accounting for the social and non-market benefits of education. In J. F. Helliwell (Ed.), *The contribution of human and social capital to sustained economic growth and well-being: International symposium report* (pp. 97–131). Paris, France: Organisation for Economic Co-operation and Development.

2

THE INCONVENIENT TRUTH ABOUT CHANGE MANAGEMENT

Why It Isn't Working and What to Do about It

SCOTT KELLER AND CAROLYN AIKEN

ABSTRACT

Conventional change management approaches have done little to change the fact that most change programs fail. The odds can be greatly improved by a number of counterintuitive insights that take into account the irrational but predictable nature of how employees interpret their environment and choose to act.

In 1995, John Kotter published what many consider to be the seminal work in the field of change management, "Leading Change: Why Transformation Efforts Fail." Kotter's (1995) "call to action" cited research that suggested only 30% of change programs are successful (p. 1). His work then went on to answer the question posed in its title and to prescribe what it takes to improve this success rate.

Kotter is perhaps the most famous purveyor of change management wisdom, but in fact he is one of many who have a point

This chapter was original published by McKinsey & Company and is reprinted here with permission. It is adapted to the format of this volume.

of view regarding how managers and companies can best manage change. In the last two decades, literally thousands of books and journal articles have been published on the topic. As of 2015, there were more than 1,900 books available on Amazon.com under the category of "organizational change." The field has developed to the extent that courses dedicated specifically to managing change are now part of the curriculum in many major MBA programs.[1]

With so much research done and information available on managing change, it stands to reason that change programs today should be more successful than those of more than a decade ago, right?

The facts suggest otherwise. McKinsey & Company recently surveyed 1,546 business executives from around the world, asking them if they consider their change programs "completely/mostly" successful: Only 30% agreed (Isern & Pung, 2006). Further investigation into a number of similar studies over the last 10 years reveals remarkably similar results.[2] The field of change management, it would seem, hasn't really changed a thing.

This failure to live up to its promise is why many senior executives today recoil at the mere mention of the words *change management*. Memories come flooding back of significant time and effort invested in the "soft stuff" that, in the end, yielded little tangible value.

The focus of McKinsey's applied research leading up to this publication has been to understand why change management efforts consistently fail to have the desired impact and, most importantly, what to do about it. At this point in our research, we don't claim to have all the answers. We have, however, developed and tested a set of perspectives in real-life application that senior managers have found genuinely insightful and that have consistently delivered business results far beyond expectations.

SUCCESSFUL CHANGE REQUIRES UNCOMMON SENSE

Digging more deeply into why change programs fail reveals that the vast majority stumble on precisely the thing they are trying to transform: employee attitudes and management behavior (vs. other possible sources such inadequate budget, poorly deployed resources, and poor change architecture; see Beer & Nohria, 2000; Caldwell, 1994; Cameron & Quinn, 1999; CSC Index, 1994; Goss, Pascale, & Athos, 1998; Kotter & Heskett, 1992).

Literally thousands of prescriptions are put forward in various change management publications regarding how to influence employee attitudes and management behavior. However, the vast majority of the thinking is remarkably similar. Price and Lawson provided a holistic perspective in their 2003 article, "The Psychology of Change Management," that suggests that four basic conditions have to be met before employees will change their behavior:

1. A compelling story: They must see the point of the change and agree with it, at least enough to give it a try

2. Role modeling: They must also see colleagues they admire modeling the desired behavior

3. Reinforcement systems: Surrounding structures, systems, processes, and incentives must be in tune with the new behavior

4. The skills required for change: They need to have the skills to do what is required of them (p. 33)

This prescription is well grounded in the field of psychology and is entirely rational. Putting all four of these conditions in place as a part of a dynamic process greatly improves the chances of bringing about lasting changes in the mindsets and behaviors of people in an organization—and thus achieves sustained improvements in business performance.

One of the merits of this approach is its intuitive appeal, so much so that many managers feel that, once revealed, it is simply good common sense. And this, we believe, is precisely where things fall apart. The prescription is right, but rational managers who attempt to put the four conditions in place by applying their "common sense" intuition typically misdirect time and energy, create messages that miss the mark, and experience frustrating unintended consequences from their efforts to influence change.

Why? In implementing the prescription, they disregard a scientific truth of human nature: People are irrational in many predictable ways. The scientific study of human irrationality has shown that many of our instincts related to understanding and influencing our own and others' motivations push us toward failure instead of success. We systematically fall victim to subconscious thought processes that significantly influence our behavior, even though our rational minds tell us they shouldn't. How many of us drive around looking for a close parking place to "save time" for longer than it would have taken to walk from the available parking spaces? How about falling into the trap of spending $3,000 to upgrade to leather seats when we buy a new $25,000 car, but finding it difficult to spend the same amount on a new leather sofa (even though we know we will spend more time on the sofa than in the car)? Are you willing to take a pencil home from work for your children to use but are not willing to raid the company's petty cash box for the money to buy a pencil for the same purpose? These examples point to how all of us are susceptible to irrationality when it comes to decision making.[3]

In the same way that the field of economics has been transformed by an improved understanding of how uniquely human social, cognitive, and emotional biases lead to seemingly irrational decisions,[4] so too the practice of change management is in need of a transformation through an improved understanding of the irrational (often unconscious) way in which humans interpret their environment and choose to act.

The scientific study of human irrationality has shown that many of our instincts related to understanding and influencing our own and others' motivations push us toward failure instead of success.

In what follows we describe a number of counterintuitive insights regarding human irrationality and implications for putting the four conditions for behavior change into place. We will also offer practical—if inconvenient—advice (as it calls for investing time and effort in areas that your rational mind will tell you shouldn't matter as much as they do) on how to improve the odds of leading successful change. We illustrate these approaches through concrete examples of how various companies have, either by conscious awareness, intuition, or simple luck, leveraged predictable employee irrationality to great effect in making change happen.

Dealing with the human side of change is not easy. As Nobel laureate Murray Gell-Mann once said, "Think how hard physics would be if particles could think." All told, we don't expect our advice to make your life as a change leader any easier. We are convinced, however, it will have more impact.

THE INCONVENIENT TRUTH ABOUT CREATING A COMPELLING STORY

Change management thinking extols the virtues of creating a compelling change story, communicating it to employees, and following it up with ongoing communications and involvement. This prescription makes sense, but in practice three inconvenient truths often get in the way of this approach achieving the desired impact.

Inconvenient Truth Number 1: What motivates you doesn't motivate (most of) your employees.

We see two types of change stories consistently told in organizations. The first is the "good-to-great" story along the lines of: "Our historical advantage has been eroded by intense competition and changing customer needs; if we change, we can regain our leadership position once again, becoming the undisputed industry leader for the foreseeable future and leaving the competition in the dust." The second is the turnaround story along the lines of: "We're performing below industry standards and must change dramatically to survive; incremental change is not sufficient—investors will not continue to put money into an underperforming company. We are capable of far more based on our assets, market position, size, skills, and loyal staff. We can become a top-quartile performer in our industry by exploiting our current assets and earning the right to grow."

These stories both seem rational, yet they too often fail to have the impact that change leaders desire. Research by a number of leading thinkers in the social sciences, such as Barrett (1998), Beck and Cowan (1996), and Zohar (1997), has shown that stories of this nature will create significant energy for change in only about 20% of your workforce. Why? The stories above all center on the company—beating the competition, industry leadership, share price targets, and so on—when in fact research shows that there are at least four other sources of meaning and motivation that can be tapped into to create energy for change: impact on society (e.g., making a better society, building the community, stewarding resources); impact on the customer (e.g., making it easier, superior service, better-quality product); impact on the working team (e.g., sense of belonging, caring environment, working together efficiently and effectively); and impact on "me" personally (e.g., my development, paycheck/bonus, empowerment to act).

The inconvenient truth about this research is that in surveys of hundreds of thousands of employees to discover which of these five (society, customer, company/shareholder, working team, "me" personally) sources of meaning most motivates them, the result is a consistently even 20% split across all dimensions. Regardless of level (senior management to the frontline), industry (health care to manufacturing), or geography (developed or developing economies), the results do not significantly differ.

This finding has profound implications for leaders. What the leader cares about (and typically bases at least 80% of his or her message to others on) does not tap into roughly 80% of the workforce's primary motivators for putting extra energy into the change program. Those people leading change should be able to tell "five stories at once" and in doing so unleash tremendous amounts of organizational energy that would otherwise remain latent in the organization.

By way of practical example, consider a cost-reduction program at a large U.S. financial services company. The program was embarked on with a rational change story that "ticked all the boxes" of conventional change management wisdom. Three months into the program, management was frustrated with the employee resistance inhibiting impact. The team worked together to recast the "story" around the cost program to include an element related to society (to deliver "affordable housing": we must be most affordable in our services); customers (increased simplicity, flexibility, fewer errors, more competitive prices); the company (expenses are growing faster than revenues, which is not sustainable); working teams (less duplication, more delegation, increased accountability, faster pace); and individuals (bigger, more attractive jobs created; a great opportunity to "make your own" institution).

This relatively simple shift in approach lifted employee motivation measures from 35.4% to 57.1% in a month, and the program went on to achieve 10% efficiency improvements in the first year—a run rate far above initial expectations.

What the leader cares about (and typically bases at least 80% of his or her message to others on) does not tap into roughly 80% of the workforce's primary motivators for putting extra energy into the change program.

Inconvenient Truth Number 2: You're better off letting them write their own story.

Well-intentioned leaders invest significant time in communicating their change story. Roadshows, town halls, magazines, screensavers, and websites are but a few of the many approaches typically used to tell the story. Certainly the story (told in five ways!) needs to get out there, but the inconvenient truth is that much of the energy invested in communicating it would be better spent listening, not telling.

In a famous experiment, researchers ran a lottery with a twist (Langer, 1982). Half the participants were randomly assigned a lottery ticket. The remaining half were given a blank piece of paper and a pen and asked to write down any number they would like as their lottery number. Just before drawing the winning number, the researchers offered to buy back the tickets from their holders. The question researchers wanted to answer is, "How much more do you have to pay someone who 'wrote their own number' versus someone who was handed a number randomly?" The rational answer would be that there is no difference (given a lottery is pure chance, and therefore every ticket number, chosen or assigned, should have the same value). A more savvy answer would be that you would have to pay less (given the possibility of duplicate numbers in the population who write their own number). The real answer? No matter what geography or demographic the experiment has taken place in, researchers have always found that they have to pay at least five times more to those who wrote their own number (Langer, 1982).

This result reveals an inconvenient truth about human nature: When we choose for ourselves, we are far more committed to the outcome (almost by a factor of five to one). Conventional approaches to change management underestimate this impact. The rational thinker sees it as a waste of time to let others self-discover what he or she already knows—why not just tell them and be done with it? Unfortunately this approach steals from others the energy needed to drive change that comes through a sense of ownership of "the answer."

Consider another practical example in Barclays' Personal Financial Services CEO David Roberts, who employed a fairly literal interpretation of the aforementioned finding. He wrote his change story in full prose, in a way that he found meaningful. He then shared it with his team, getting feedback on what resonated and what needed further clarification. He then asked each of his team members to "write their own lottery ticket": What was the change story for them, in their business, that supports the bigger PFS-wide change story? His team members wrote their change story, again in full prose, and shared it with their teams. Their teams gave feedback and then wrote their own story for their area/department, and so the process continued all the way to the frontline. It took twice as long as the traditional road-show approach, but for a five-times return on commitment to the program, it was the right investment to make.[5]

> **When we choose for ourselves, we are far more committed to the outcome (almost by a factor of five to one).**

Sam Palmisano, former CEO of IBM, in spearheading a change effort to move IBM toward a values-based management system, enabled thousands of employees to "write their own lottery ticket" regarding IBM's values. During a three-day, online discussion forum (dubbed "ValuesJam"), over 50,000 employees were empowered literally to rewrite IBM's century-old values (Hemp & Stewart, 2004).

Other applications need not be so literal. At a global consumer goods company, the CEO brought together his top 300 for three two-day "real work" sessions over three months where they created the story together. Again, this process invested significant time, but having the top 300 five-times committed to the way forward was considered well worth the investment (Priestland & Hanig, 2005). At BP, to develop a comprehensive training program for frontline leaders, a decision was made to involve every key constituency in the design of the program, giving them a sense of "writing their own lottery ticket." It took a year and a half to complete the design using this model but was well worth it. Now in implementation, the program is the highest rated of its kind in BP. It involves more than 250 active senior managers from across the business willingly teaching the course, and, most importantly, has resulted in managers who have been through the training program being consistently ranked higher in performance than those who haven't, both by their bosses and by the employees who report to them (Priestland & Hanig, 2005).

At a minimum, we advocate that leaders leverage the "lottery ticket" insight by augmenting their telling of the story with *asking* about the story. Consider David Farr, CEO of Emerson Electric, who is noted for asking four questions related to his company's story of virtually everyone he encounters in the organization: (1) How do you make a difference? (testing for alignment on the company's direction); (2) What improvement idea are you working on? (emphasizing continuous improvement); (3) When did you last get coaching from your boss? (emphasizing the importance of people development); and (4) Who is the enemy? (emphasizing the importance of "One Emerson"/no silos; i.e., he wanted to emphasize the "right" answer was the competition and not some other department!) (Keller & Price, 2011).

On a final note, many executives are surprised not only by the ownership and drive for implementation that comes from high-involvement approaches but also by the improved quality of the answers that emerge. As one CEO told us, "I was surprised how people stepped up during the direction-setting process—I was worried about everything getting 'dumbed down,' but in the end we got a better answer because of the broad involvement."

*Inconvenient Truth Number 3: It takes both "+" and "–"
to create real energy.*

In 210 BC, a Chinese commander named Xiang Yu led his troops across the Yangtze River to attack the army of the Qin (Ch'in) dynasty. Camped for the night on the banks of the river, his troops awakened to find their ships on fire. They rushed to the boats ready to take on their attackers, only to find that it was Xiang Yu himself who had set their ships ablaze. Not only that, but he had also ordered all the cooking pots crushed. Xiang Yu's logic was that without the pots and the ships, they had no other choice but to fight their way to victory or die trying. In doing so, he created tremendous focus in his troops, who battled ferociously against the enemy and won nine consecutive battles, obliterating the main-force units of the Qin dynasty.

This story is perhaps the ultimate example of creating a "burning platform" to motivate action—a message that says, "We've got a problem, we have to change!" This model is often referred to as a deficit-based approach to change. It identifies the problem (What is the need?), analyzes causes (What is wrong here?) and possible solutions (How can we fix it?), and then plans and takes actions (Problem solved!). Advocates of this approach point out that its linear logic and approach to dissecting things to understand them is at the heart of all the scientific progress made by Western civilization. They also cite examples like that of Xiang Yu, where it has a profound effect. Given the case for the deficit-based approach, it has become the model predominantly taught in business schools and is presumably the default change model in most organizations. At success rates of 30%, however, the vast majority of change leaders are not enjoying the same success as Xiang Yu did. Why is this?

Research has shown that a relentless focus on "what's wrong" is not sustainable, invokes blame, and creates fatigue and resistance, doing little to engage people's passion and experience and highlight their success. This result has led to the rise of what many refer to as the constructionist-based approach to change. In this approach the change process is based on discovery (discovering the best of what is), dreaming (imagining what might be), designing (talking about what should be), and destiny (creating what will be).[6]

Consider a study done at the University of Wisconsin where two bowling teams were recorded on video over a number of games. Each team received a video to study. One team's video showed only those occasions when it made mistakes. The other's showed only those occasions when it performed well. The team that studied its successes improved its score twice as much as the other team. The conclusion is that choosing the positive as the focus of inquiry and storytelling is the best answer for creating change (Mohr & Watkins, 2002). Whereas the deficit-based change approach is well suited for technical systems, research into the constructionist-based approach shows that in human systems a focus on "what's right" can achieve improved results. So should enlightened change leaders shift their focus exclusively to capturing opportunities and building on strengths instead of identifying and solving problems? We think not.

Humans are more risk averse when choosing among options framed as "gains" than when they choose among those framed as "losses." For example, what would you do if given the choice between a sure gain of $100 and a 50% chance of gaining $200? Social science experiments show that most individuals are risk averse and take the gain. What would you do if given the choice between a sure loss of $100 or a 50% chance of losing $200? If you are like most individuals, you are risk seeking in this case and choose a 50% chance of losing $200 (Burnham & Phelan, 2000). A single-minded focus on "what's possible," with its bias toward more conservative choices, flies in the face of achieving radical change. The reason for this is that, as humans, we inherently dislike losses more than we like gains.[7]

The inconvenient truth is that both the deficit-based and constructionist approaches to change have their merits and limitations. It is clear that a single-minded focus on today's problems creates more fatigue and resistance than envisioning a positive future. But it is also clear that when it comes to behavioral change, some

> **It is clear that a single-minded focus on today's problems creates fatigue and resistance. . . . But it is also clear that when it comes to behavioral change, some anxiety is good.**

anxiety is good, and that an overemphasis on the positive can lead to watered-down aspirations and impact.

We believe the field of change management has drawn an artificial divide between deficit-based and constructionist-based approaches. The best answer is an "and" answer. While it is impossible to prescribe generally how the divide should be split between positive and negative messages, as this will be specific to the context of any given change program, we strongly advise managers not to "swing the pendulum" too far in one direction or another. Consider Jack Welch at GE, who took head-on the question of "What's wrong here?" (poorly performing businesses, impending bankruptcy, silo-driven behaviors, bureaucracy, etc.) as well as "imagining what might be" (number one or two in every business, a "boundaryless" culture of quality, openness, account-ability, etc.).

Revisiting the University of Wisconsin bowling team experiment mentioned earlier, we suspect that a team that studied its successes *and* mistakes would outperform teams that studied only either/or.

THE INCONVENIENT TRUTH ABOUT ROLE MODELING

Conventional change management suggests leaders should take actions that role model the desired change and mobilize a group of influence leaders to drive change deep into the organization. Unfortunately, this prescription rarely delivers the desired impact because it neglects two more inconvenient truths about change management.

Inconvenient Truth Number 4: Your leaders believe they already "are the change."

Most senior executives understand and generally buy into Gandhi's famous aphorism, "Be the change you want to see in the world." They, often prompted by HR professionals or consultants, commit themselves to "being the change" by personally role modeling the desired behaviors. And then, in practice, nothing significant changes.

The reason for this outcome is that most executives don't see themselves as "part of the problem" and therefore deep down do not believe that it is *they* who need to change, even though in principle they agree that leaders must role model the desired changes. Take for example a team that reports that, as a group and as an organization, they are low in trust, not customer-focused, and bureaucratic. How many executives when asked privately will say "no" to the questions "Do you consider yourself to be trustworthy?" and "Are you customer focused?" and "yes" to the question "Are you a bureaucrat?" Of course, none.

The fact is that most well-intentioned and hard-working people believe they are doing the right thing, or they wouldn't be doing it. However, most people also have an unwarranted optimism in relation to their own behavior. Consider that 94% of men rank themselves in the top half of male athletic ability. Of course this is irrational, as mathematically exactly 50% of males are in the top half of male athletic ability. This tendency isn't only true for males and athletics—far more than 50% of people rank themselves in the top half of driving ability, although it is a statistical impossibility. When couples are asked to estimate their contribution to household work, the combined total routinely exceeds 100%. In many behavior-related areas, human beings consistently think they are better than they are—a phenomenon referred to in psychology as a "self-serving bias" (Barber & Odean, 2001; Ross & Sicoly, 1979; Svenson, 1981). Whereas conventional change management approaches surmise that top team role modeling is a matter of will ("wanting to change") or skill ("knowing how to change"), the inconvenient truth is that the real bottleneck to role modeling is knowing "what" to change at a personal level.

Typically, insight into "what" to change can be created by concrete 360-degree feedback techniques via surveys, conversations, or both. This 360-degree feedback should not be against generic HR leadership competency models but, instead, against the specific behaviors related to the desired changes that will drive business performance. This style of feedback can be augmented by fact gathering such as third-party observation of senior

The fact is that most well-intentioned and hard-working people believe they are doing the right thing, or they wouldn't be doing it. However, most people also have an unwarranted optimism in relation to their own behavior.

executives going about their day-to-day work (e.g., "You say you are not bureaucratic, but every meeting you are in creates three additional meetings and no decisions are made") and calendar analyses (e.g., "You say you are customer focused but have spent 5% of your time reviewing customer-related data and no time meeting with customers or customer-facing employees").

Consider Amgen CEO Kevin Sharer's approach of asking each of his top 75, "What should I do differently?" and sharing his development needs and commitment publicly with them (McKinsey & Company Organization Practice, 2013). Consider the top team of a national insurance company who routinely employed what they called the "circle of fire" during their change program: Every participant receives feedback live in the room, directly from their colleagues on "What makes you great?" in relation to "being the change" and "What makes you small?" Consider the leadership coalition (top 25) of a multiregional bank who, after each major event in their change program, conducted a short, targeted 360-degree feedback survey regarding how well their behaviors role modeled the desired behaviors during the event, ensuring that feedback was timely, relevant, and practical (McKinsey & Company Organization Practice, 2013).

While seemingly inconvenient, these types of techniques help break through the "self-serving bias" that inhibits well-meaning leaders from making a profound difference through their actions to the ultimate impact of the change program.

Note that some readers may be thinking, "But surely there are a few people who *are* fully role modeling the desired behaviors— what does this mean for them?" If the purpose of senior executive role modeling is to exhibit the behaviors required that ensure the success and sustainability of the change program (e.g., collaboration, agility in decision making, empowerment), then the answer is "Keep up the good work!" If the answer, however, is expanded to include role modeling the process of personal behavioral change itself, there is more to do. Recall that Gandhi also said famously, "For things to change, first I must change."

We often cite Tiger Woods's reaction to his astonishing, 18-below-par victory in the Masters tournament in 1997: he chose to rebuild his swing. As he practiced many of its 270 elements, he endured a period of awkward performance. The press deemed him a one-Masters wonder. Four years later, he won the world's four major golf tournaments in one year, an unprecedented accomplishment. At one point, Woods's lead over the second-ranked player was larger than the gap between number 2 and number 100.[8] The lesson is clear: Continued success requires critical self-examination and growth. Few senior executives would suggest they are less in need of personal learning than Tiger Woods.

Inconvenient Truth Number 5: Influence leaders aren't that influential.

Almost all change management literature places importance on mobilizing a set of "influence leaders" to help drive the change. Typically guidance is given to find and mobilize those in the organization who either by role or personality (or both) have disproportionate influence over how others think and behave. We believe this is sound and timeless advice—indeed having a cadre of well-regarded people proactively role modeling and communicating the change program is a "no-regrets" move. However, since Malcolm Gladwell (2000) popularized his "law of the few" in his best-selling book *The Tipping Point*, we have observed that the role of influence leaders has moved from being perceived as a helpful element of a broader set of interventions to a panacea for making change happen (likely an unintended consequence of Gladwell's work, which itself was directed toward marketers vs. change leaders).

   Gladwell's (2000) "law of the few" suggests that rare, highly connected people shape the world. He defined three types of influence leaders that are among this select group: mavens, who are discerning individuals who accumulate knowledge and share advice; connectors, or those who know lots of people; and salespeople, who are those who have the natural ability to influence and persuade others. Gladwell illustrated his point with the example of Hush Puppies. The footwear brand was dying by late 1994—until a few New York hipsters began wearing their shoes. Other fashionistas followed suit, whereupon the cool kids copied them, the less-cool kids copied them, and so on, until voilà! Within two years, sales of Hush Puppies had exploded by 5,000%, without a penny spent on advertising (Gladwell, 2000). Compelling stories such as this have been interpreted by many change leaders as evidence that the lion's share of their role should focus on getting the influence leader equation right and—voilà!—all else will follow.

Duncan Watts, a network-theory scientist working for Yahoo!, has conducted a number of experiments that help explain why "influence leaders" are not the panacea the aforementioned example implies. In the context of the Hush Puppies story, he essentially posed the more expansive question, "Given East Village hipsters were wearing lots of cool things in the fall of 1994, why did only Hush Puppies take off? Why didn't their other clothing choices reach a tipping point too?" His research shows that influence leaders are no more likely to start a social "contagion" than the rank and file. He concludes that success depends less on how persuasive the "early adopter" is and more on how receptive the "society" is to the idea. To start a social epidemic is less a matter of finding the mavens, connectors, and salespeople to do the infecting and more a matter of developing the "virus" that society is a fertile spreading ground for. Watts suggested a better metaphor than a virus—a forest fire—for the way social influence really works. There are thousands of forest fires a year, but only a few become roaring monsters. Why? Because in those rare situations the landscape is ripe: sparse rain, dry woods, badly equipped fire departments. In these situations, no one will go around talking about the exceptional properties of the random smoker who unwittingly tossed a smoldering cigarette butt into a patch of parched grass in the middle of a forest during a drought (Thompson, 2008).

> **Influence leaders are no more likely to start a social "contagion" than the rank and file. . . . Success depends less on how persuasive the "early adopter" is and more on how receptive the "society" is to the idea.**

The inconvenient truth is that it is not enough to invest in a few rather than in many as a way of catalyzing desired changes, no matter how appealing the idea is. We warn against overestimating the impact a group of influence leaders can have and, in turn, overinvesting in them in a world of scarce resources (time, money, people). We advocate that change leader attention should be balanced across all four conditions for change—a compelling story, role modeling, reinforcement systems, and the skills required for change—to ensure they are reinforcing in ways that maximize the probability of the change "spark" taking off like wildfire across the organization.

THE INCONVENIENT TRUTH ABOUT REINFORCING MECHANISMS

Conventional change management emphasizes the importance of reinforcing and embedding desired changes in structures, processes, systems, target setting, and incentives. If you want collaboration, create cross-functional teams. If you want customer focus, make sure your systems give you a full picture of the customer relationship. If you want just about any behavior, make people's paychecks dependent on it, and so the logic goes. Again, these are all perfectly rational until confronted with two inconvenient truths.

Inconvenient Truth Number 6: Money is the most expensive way to motivate people.

Upton Sinclair once wrote, "It is difficult to get a man to understand something if his salary depends upon him not understanding it."[9] If a change program's objectives are not linked somehow to employee compensation, this sends a strong message that the change program is not a priority, and motivation for change is adversely affected. The flip side, however, is not true. When change program objectives are linked to compensation, motivation for change is rarely meaningfully enhanced. The reason for this phenomenon is as practical as it is psychological in nature.

Consider the change manager who is working to link the change program with compensation. He or she is faced with existing executives' annual compensation plan that is typically comprised of three elements: a portion dependent on how the corporation does (typically an earnings or return-on-capital number for the whole company); a portion dependent on how the leader's specific business or function does; and a portion dependent on individual goals, often related to operations or people.

The rational change manager dutifully builds change program impact into earnings forecasts and business unit/functional financial operating plans. Come review time, however, he or she realizes that with the myriad controllable and uncontrollable variables that influence the financial outcomes, the link to specific change program implementation becomes weak at best. Operational (nonfinancial) impact from change program implementation creates a stronger link to outcomes and individual efforts. Unfortunately, however, the weighting of nonfinancial outcomes from the change program in the context of the vast array of other metrics also "linked" to rewards (e.g., compliance, safety, social responsibility, diversity, talent development, leadership competencies) renders any link to compensation hardly relevant.

The reality is that in the vast majority of companies, it is exceedingly difficult to meaningfully link a change program to individual compensation. So why not just change the compensation approach? This strategy is of course an option, but it is easier said than done and is certainly not without risk and potential unintended consequences when considering that change must happen in real time— the organization must continue to carry out its day-to-day tasks and functions while at the same time fundamentally rethinking them. The good news is that there are easier, relatively inexpensive ways to use incentives to motivate employees for change.

In one study, researchers gave people a tiny gift and measured the increase in satisfaction with their lives. Specifically, half of a group of people who used a photocopier found a dime in the coin return. How much did the gift increase their satisfaction with their lives? When asked about how satisfied they were with their lives, those with the dime were 6.5 on a 7 scale, whereas those without were only 5.6 (Schwartz, 1987). Why such a lift in satisfaction for such little reward? For human beings, it holds that satisfaction equals perception minus expectation (an equation often accompanied by the commentary "reality has nothing to do with it"). The beauty of this equation for change managers is that small, unexpected rewards can have disproportionate effects on employees' "satisfaction" with a change program.

Gordon M. Bethune, while turning around Continental Airlines, sent an unexpected $65 check to every employee when Continental made it to the top 5 for on-time airlines. John McFarlane of ANZ Bank sent a bottle of champagne to every employee for Christmas with a card thanking them for their work on the company's "Perform, Grow and Breakout" change program. The CEO of a large multiregional bank sent out personal thank-you notes to all employees working directly on the company's change program to mark its first-year anniversary (Aiken & Keller, 2009). Most change managers would refer to these as merely token gestures and argue that their impact is limited and short-lived. Employees on the receiving end beg to differ. Recipients of these "dime-in-the-photocopier" equivalents consistently report back that the rewards have a disproportionately positive

For human beings, it holds that satisfaction equals perception minus expectation— small, unexpected rewards can have disproportionate effects.

impact on change motivation that lasts for months, if not years.

The reason these small, unexpected rewards have such impact is because employees perceive them as a "social exchange" with the company versus a "market exchange." To understand the difference, consider the following. Assume you are at your mother-in-law's house for Thanksgiving dinner. She has spent weeks planning the meal and all day cooking. After the meal you thank her and ask her how much you should pay for the experience. What would her reaction be? Most people report that their mother-in-law would be horrified and the relationship damaged as a result. Why? The offer of money takes the interaction from a social norm, built around a reciprocal, long-term relationship, to a market norm that is more transactional and shallow. Back to your mother-in-law, would she have accepted a nice bottle of wine for the table as a gift from you? Likely, yes, as small, unexpected gifts indicate social norms are at play.[10]

Consider the study of a daycare center where a $3 fine was imposed for parents picking up their children late (Dubner & Levitt, 2005). When the fine went into place, incidents of late pickups went through the roof. Why? Before the fine was imposed, the daycare staff and the parents had a social contract—for the parents, feeling guilty about being late compelled them to be more prompt in picking up their kids. Once the fine was imposed, the daycare center had inadvertently replaced social norms with market norms. Free from feelings of guilt, parents frequently chose to be late and pay the fee (certainly not what the center had intended!).

When it comes to change, social norms are not only cheaper than market norms but often more effective as well. By way of example, consider the American Association of Retired Persons (AARP), which asked some lawyers if they would offer less expensive services to needy retirees, at something like $30 an hour. The lawyers said no. Then the program manager from AARP had the idea to ask the lawyers if they would offer free services for needy retirees. Overwhelmingly, the lawyers said yes. When compensation was mentioned, the lawyers applied market norms and found the offer lacking. When no compensation was mentioned, they used social norms and were willing to volunteer their time (Ariely, 2008).

Inconvenient Truth Number 7: A fair process is as important as a fair outcome.

Consider a bank that, as part of a major change program, diagnosed that its pricing did not appropriately reflect the credit risk that the institution was taking on. New risk-adjusted rate of return (or RAROC-based) models were created, and the resulting new pricing schedules delivered to the frontline. At the same time, sales incentives were adjusted to reward customer profitability versus volume. The result? Customer attrition (not only of the unprofitable ones) and price overrides went through the roof, and, ultimately, significant value was destroyed by the effort. The rational change manager scratches his or her head in confusion wondering, "What went wrong?"

"Ultimatum games" offer a compelling example of the inconvenient truth at play here. Give a stranger $10. Tell them they must split the money with another stranger however they wish. If the person accepts the offer, the money is split. If they reject the offer, no one gets any money. Studies show that if the offer is a $7.50/$2.50 split, more than 95 percent will reject it, preferring to go home with nothing than to see someone "unfairly" receive three times as much as they do.[11] You may be thinking to yourself that with a total pie of $10 to share, unequal allocations are rejected only because the absolute amount of the offer is low. Seemingly irrationally, however, the "ultimatum game" findings are the same even when the absolute amount of the offer is equivalent to two weeks of wages (Cameron, 1999).[12]

The inconvenient truth is that employees will go against their own self-interest (read: incentives) if the situation violates other notions they have about the way the world should work, in particular, in relation to fairness and justice. In the case of the banking price rise example described earlier, whether right or wrong, the frontline view of the pricing and incentive changes was that they were unfair to the customer, a symbol of increasingly greedy executives losing sight of customer service. Even though it meant they were less likely to achieve their individual sales goals, a significant number of bankers vocally bad-mouthed the bank's policies to customers, putting themselves on the customer's side rather than the bank's. Where possible, price overrides were then used to show good faith to customers and inflict retribution on the "greedy" executives.

In making any changes to company structures, processes, systems, and incentives, change managers should pay an unreasonable amount of attention to employees' sense of the fairness of the change process as well as the outcome. Particular care should be taken where changes affect how employees interact with one another (headcount reductions, changes to processes such as talent management, annual planning, etc.) and with customers (sales stimulation programs, call center redesigns, pricing, etc.). Ironically, in the pricing example described previously, the outcome is inherently fair (customers are asked to pay commensurate to the risk the bank is taking on), and therefore the downward spiral described could have been avoided (and has been by other banks adopting

Employees will go against their own self-interest (read: incentives) if the situation violates other notions they have about the way the world should work, in particular, in relation to fairness and justice.

RAROC-based pricing) by carefully tending to employees' perceptions of fairness in the communications and training surrounding the changes.

THE INCONVENIENT TRUTH ABOUT CAPABILITY BUILDING

Conventional change management emphasizes the importance of building the skills and talent needed for the desired change to be successful and sustainable. Though hard to argue with, in practice there are two more inconvenient truths that demand attention if one is to successfully build the needed capabilities.

Inconvenient Truth Number 8: Employees are what they think.

Many managers believe in their heart of hearts that the soft stuff—employees' thoughts, feelings, and beliefs—has no place in workplace dialog. "All that matters is that they behave in the ways I need them to; it doesn't matter why," they will say. While rational—behaviors drive performance, after all—this view misses the point that it is employees' thoughts, feelings, and beliefs that drive their behaviors. Ignoring the underlying mindsets of employees during change is to address symptoms rather than root causes.

Consider an analogy from operations management. When a motor burns out on a machine on the shop floor, it is replaced, right? Effective managers will only replace the engine once the root causes are known: "Why did the motor burn out?" Because it overheated. "Why did it overheat?" Because it was insufficiently ventilated. "Why was it insufficiently ventilated?" Because the machine is too close to the wall. The operator then moves the machine away from the wall and replaces the motor. Not doing so would mean the fix would be short-lived (the new motor would have quickly burned out, too, due to the lack of ventilation). A far better solution is achieved by addressing the root cause.

Let's see how this applies to change management. Consider a bank that through a benchmarking exercise found that its sales per banker were lagging behind the competition. "Why are sales per banker lower?," the rational manager asks. Analysis shows bankers are not spending enough time with customers. "Why aren't they spending more time with customers?" Because a significant amount of their time is spent completing paperwork. With this diagnosis, the bank set about reengineering the loan-origination process to minimize paperwork and maximize customer-facing time. Not only that, bankers are provided with new sales scripts and easier-to-use tools so that they'll know what to do with the extra time in front of the customer.

Ignoring the underlying mindsets of employees during change is to address symptoms rather than root causes.

Training on the new processes and tools is administered and, voilà, problem solved. Except for the fact that six months later, the levels of improvement are far lower than envisioned.

What went wrong? A further investigation into "why," with an eye to the bankers' mindsets, provides a much fuller view of the root causes: Is there anything about how they think and feel, or what they believe about themselves and their jobs, that explains why they wouldn't be spending more time with customers? Faced with a stalled improvement program, the bank in question proceeded down this line of inquiry. They quickly found that most of the bankers in question simply found customer interactions uncomfortable and therefore actually preferred paperwork to interacting with people (and, in turn, created reasons not to spend time with customers). This situation was driven by a combination of introvert personalities, poor interpersonal skills, and a feeling of inferiority when dealing with customers who by and large have more money and education than they do. Furthermore, supervisors (who had mostly been recruited from the banker ranks) were also insecure with their selling and interpersonal skills and therefore placed more emphasis on managing paper-based activity, further exacerbating the problem. Finally, most bankers were loath to think of themselves as "salespeople"—a notion they perceived as better suited to employees on used car lots than in bank branches. Efforts to create "more sales time" flew directly in the face of their vocational identity.

Armed with these root cause insights, the bank's change program was enhanced to directly address the mindset challenges as well as the process and tool barriers. Training for bankers and supervisors was expanded to include elements related to personality types, emotional intelligence, and vocational identity (recasting "sales" as the more noble pursuit of "helping customers discover and fulfill their unarticulated needs"). This enhancement not only put the program back on track within six months but also ultimately delivered sustainable sales lifts in excess of original targets.

Those skeptical of the importance of mindsets are encouraged to consider the Roger Bannister story. Until 1954, the four-minute mile was considered to be beyond human achievement. Medical journals of the day went so far as to declare it an impossible "behavior." In May of that year, however, Roger Bannister broke this barrier, running the mile in 3 minutes, 59.4 seconds. What is perhaps more amazing is that two months later it was broken again, by Australian John Landy. And within three years, 16 other runners had also broken this record. What happened? A sudden spurt in human evolution? Genetic engineering of a new super race of runners? Of course not. It was the same human equipment but with a different mindset—one that said "this can be done."

Bannister emphasized in his memoirs that he spent as much time conditioning his mind as he did conditioning his body. He wrote, "the mental approach is all important . . . energy can be harnessed by the correct attitude of mind" (Bannister, 1981, p. 210). While perhaps inconvenient, when it comes to building capabilities required for change, we believe a balance should be struck between building technical skills and shifting underlying mindsets (to enable the technical skills to be used to their fullest).

Inconvenient Truth Number 9: Good intentions aren't enough.

It is well documented that after three months adults retain only 10% of what they have heard in lecture-based training sessions (e.g., presentations, videos, demonstrations, discussions). When they learn by doing (e.g., role plays, simulations, case studies), 65% of the learning is retained. And when they practice what they have learned in the workplace for a number of weeks, almost all of the learning can be expected to be retained (Whitmore, 2004). Accordingly, effective skill-building programs are replete with interactive simulations and role plays to ensure time spent in the training room is most effective. Further, commitments are made by participants regarding what they will "practice" back in the workplace ("My Monday morning takeaway is . . .") to embed the learnings. This is all well and good, except that come Monday morning, very few keep their commitments.

Consider a social science experiment at a Princeton theological seminary. Students were asked a series of questions about their personality and level of religious commitment and then sent across campus. Along the way, they met a person slumped over coughing and groaning and asking for medical assistance. Did self-proclaimed nice people help more? Absolutely not. Neither did religious commitment correlate to who provided help. The only predictor of the seminarians' behavior was that half were made to think they were late for an appointment across campus, while the others believed they had plenty of time. Sixty-three percent with spare time helped, as opposed to just 10% of those in a hurry. When short of time, even those with "religion as a quest" did not stop to help (Darley & Batson, 1973).

Given this aspect of human nature, it is unreasonable to expect that most employees will genuinely practice new skills and behaviors back in the workplace if nothing formal has been done to lower the barriers to doing so. The time and energy required to do something additional, or even to do something in a new way, simply do not exist in busy executives' day-to-day schedules. Ironically, this is particularly the case in the days following training programs, when most managers are playing catch-up from their time away. This failure to formalize and create the space for practice back in the workplace dooms most training programs to deliver returns that are at best 65% of their potential.

We advocate a number of enhancements to traditional training approaches to "hardwire" day-to-day practice into capability-building processes. First, training should not be a one-off event. Instead, a "field and forum" approach should be taken, in which classroom training is spread over a series of learning forums and fieldwork is assigned in between. Second, we suggest creating fieldwork assignments that link directly to the day jobs of participants, requiring them to put into practice new mindsets and skills in ways that are

Failure to formalize and create the space for practice back in the workplace dooms most training programs to deliver returns that are at best 65% of their potential.

"hardwired" into the things for which they are accountable. These assignments should have quantifiable, outcome-based measures that indicate levels of competence gained and certification that recognizes and rewards the skills attained.

Consider one company's approach to building lean manufacturing capabilities. The first forum offered a core of basic skills and mindsets in performance improvement. Fieldwork then followed, involving cost, quality, and service improvement targets over a three-month period. Anyone delivering on these targets was awarded a green-belt certification in lean. The next forum provided much deeper technical system design skills and project and team leadership training. The fieldwork that followed involved participants redesigning entire areas of the plant floor and overseeing a portfolio of specific improvement teams, all aspects of which had quantitative targets (both in terms of financial results and people and project leadership in 360-degree evaluations). Anyone achieving their fieldwork targets then became a black belt in lean. The final forum built more advanced skills in shaping plant-wide improvement programs in the context of pressing strategic issues, applying improvement concepts to more complex operations, and coaching and mentoring others. Fieldwork again put these lessons into practice with quantitative improvement goals attached, resulting in a set of "master black belts" emerging from the program.

SHOW ME THE MONEY!

So far, we have tested the incremental impact of applying these inconvenient truths in practice above and beyond more conventional approaches to influencing behavior in three longitudinal studies. Each study has employed control versus experimental group methodologies (comparing impact with like customer and employee demographics, ensuring minimal distortions of trial over a one-year test period). In each of these cases, the results have been profound.

In retail banking, for example, applying conventional change management approaches in a salesforce stimulation program achieved an 8% lift in profit per business banker and 7% per retail banker. While respectable, this result was below management aspirations of achieving a 10% lift in both areas. Where inconvenient truths were acted on beyond conventional change management approaches, however, the program achieved a 19% lift in profit per business banker and 12% per retail banker, far exceeding management's expectations.[13]

In the call centers of a large telecommunications company, the results of a customer churn reduction program applying conventional change management approaches resulted in 35% churn reduction, falling short of management's aspiration of a 50% reduction. Acting on the inconvenient truths, however, delivered 65% churn reduction to the delight of management, employees, and customers.

An insurance back office that had implemented lean operations improvements found that performance six months after the "step change" was stagnant, not fulfilling the continuous improvement expectations of the program. Revamping the program to leverage inconvenient truths, the company has now posted more than two years of 5% improvement (above and beyond the step change) in cost, quality, and service, exceeding the 3% continuous improvement target built into the budget.

As mentioned earlier, we acknowledge that our research into the impact of applying approaches based on the inconvenient truths about change management is still in its relatively early days by virtue of the fact that sustainable impact can only be measured over numbers of years. The aforementioned longitudinal examples, however, give us confidence and motivation to broadly share the thinking.

David Whyte (1996) once wrote, "Work, paradoxically, does not ask enough of us, yet exhausts the narrow part of us we bring to the door" (p. 22). Our research and experience have led us to believe that the impact of conventional change management thinking is held back by exactly this paradox. More activity is undertaken, less energy is tapped into, and ultimately change impact is disappointing. By acting on the inconvenient truths discussed here, Whyte's paradox is at least in part resolved by tapping into motivations that are uniquely human. In doing so, tremendous individual and organizational energy for change is unleashed.

NOTES

1. Examples include Harvard, Managing Change; Michigan, Navigating Change; MIT, Planning and Managing and Change; Duke, Human Assets and Organizational Change; Columbia, Organizational Change; IMD (Switzerland), Managing Change; London Business School (United Kingdom), Managing Change; INSEAD (France/Singapore), Leadership & Change; ESADE I (France), Change Management; Queens University (Canada), Strategy Implementation & Change Management.
2. Miller (2002) reported that 70% of change programs fail, and Higgs and Rowland (2005) reported, "Only one in four or five change programs actually succeed" (p. 125).
3. The leather seats and pencil examples have been borrowed from Ariely (2008).
4. Behavioral economics and behavioral finance are closely related fields that apply scientific research on human and social cognitive and emotional biases to better understand economic decisions and how they affect market prices, returns, and the allocation of resources. Daniel Kahneman, with Amos Tversky and others, established a cognitive basis for common human errors using heuristics and biases (Kahneman & Tversky, 1973; Kahneman, Slovic, & Tversky, 1982), and developed prospect theory (Kahneman & Tversky, 1979). Kahneman was awarded the 2002 Nobel Prize in economics for his work in prospect theory as a psychologically realistic alternative to expected utility theory.
5. See Barclays' Personal Financial Services CEO David Roberts (2002, April). "Easy to Do Business With: The Way Ahead for PFS."
6. This juxtaposition of the deficit-based and constructionist-based approaches to change is taken directly from Mohr and Watkins (2002).
7. For further evidence that humans are "irrational" loss avoiders, see Kahneman and Tversky (1984).

8. Note that in an interview with *Time* published August 14, 2000, looking back on his decision, he told writer Dan Goodgame: "I know I wasn't in the greatest position with my swing at the [1997] Masters. But my timing was great, so I got away with it. And I made almost every putt. You can have a wonderful week like that even when your swing isn't sound. But can you still contend in tournaments with that swing when your timing isn't as good? Will it hold up over a long period of time? The answer to those questions, with the swing I had, was 'no.' And I wanted to change that." Rankings reported by Harig (2004).

9. Sinclair recalled this statement from his 1934 California gubernatorial campaign speeches in his memoir (Sinclair, 1935, p. 109).

10. The "mother-in-law" example has been borrowed from Ariely (2008, p. 72).

11. The seminal ultimatum game study is by Güth, Schmittberger, and Schwarze (1982). Note that new ultimatum game research in the field of neuroeconomics shows us exactly what part of the brain operates the bilateral anterior insula (not part of the prefrontal cortex) in rejecting small offers (Sanfey, Rilling, Aronson, Nystrom, & Cohen, 2003).

12. This assumption was also tested by having U.S. participants play the game for $100. They found no difference between play for $100 and play for $10 (Hoffman, McCabe, & Smith, 1996).

13. Experimental and control group clusters of bank branches were chosen that matched each other and the organizational average on three dimensions: (1) performance: NPBT (growth and average over longest coherent period available), economics of customers, average income per customer, industry composition in business banks (split between service and manufacturing industry), and characteristics of centers; (2) staff: performance rating, tenure (+2.5 years min.); and (3) size: footings per banker. During the study we ensured no distortions of trial occurred in terms of change of management, restructuring of operations, and test of other initiatives in an incomplete subset of trial participants. Performance was compared over one year between three groups: (1) no intervention, (2) salesforce effectiveness

improvement program with "rational" change management interventions, and (3) salesforce effectiveness improvement program with "rational" change management interventions. This approach is illustrative of all longitudinal studies mentioned. (See, for example, Güth, Schmittberger, and Schwarze, 1982; Hoffman, McCabe, & Smith, 1996; Sanfey et al., 2003).

REFERENCES

Aiken, C., & Keller, S. (2009). The irrational side of change management. *McKinsey Quarterly*. Retrieved May 15, 2015 from http://www.mckinsey.com/insights/organization/the_irrational_side_of_change_management

Ariely, D. (2008). *Predictably irrational: The hidden forces that shape our decisions.* New York, NY: HarperCollins.

Bannister, R. (1981). *The four-minute mile.* Guilford, CT: Lyons Press.

Barber, B. M., & Odean, T. (2001). Boys will be boys: Gender, overconfidence, and common stock investment. *Quarterly Journal of Economics 116*, 261–292. doi:10.1162/003355301556400

Barrett, R. (1998). *Liberating the corporate soul: Building a visionary organization.* Boston, MA: Butterworth-Heinemann.

Beck, D., & Cowan, C. (1996). *Spiral dynamics: Mastering values, leadership, and change.* Cambridge, MA: Blackwell Business.

Beer, M., & Nohria, N. (Eds.). (2000). *Breaking the code of change.* Cambridge, MA: Harvard Business School Press.

Burnham, T., & Phelan, J. (2000). *Mean genes: From sex to money to food, taming our primal instincts.* Cambridge, MA: Perseus.

Caldwell, B. (1994, June 20). Missteps, miscues: Business re-engineering failures have cost corporations billions, and spending is still on the rise. *Information Week*, 50–60.

Cameron, K. S., & Quinn, R. E. (1999). *Diagnosing and changing organizational culture: Based on the competing values framework.* Reading, MA: Addison-Wesley.

Cameron, L. (1999). Raising the stakes in the ultimatum game: Experimental evidence from Indonesia. *Economic Inquiry 37*, 47–59. doi:10.1111/j.1465-7295.1999.tb01415.x

CSC Index. (1994). *CSC index state of reengineering report: North America and Europe.* Cambridge, MA: Author.

Darley, J. M., & Batson, C. D. (1973). From Jerusalem to Jericho: A study of situational and dispositional variables in helping behavior. *Journal of Personality and Social Psychology 27*, 100–108. doi:10.1037/h0034449

Dubner, S. J., & Levitt, S. D. (2005). *Freakonomics: A rogue economist explores the hidden side of everything.* New York, NY: William Morrow.

Gladwell, M. (2000). *The tipping point: How little things can make a big difference.* Boston, MA: Little, Brown.

Goss, T., Pascale, R. T., & Athos, A. (1998). The reinvention roller coaster: Risking the present for a powerful future. *Harvard Business Review 71*(6), 97–107.

Güth, W., Schmittberger, R., & Schwarze, B. (1982). An experimental analysis of ultimatum bargaining. *Journal of Economic Behavior and Organization 3*, 367–388. doi:10.1016/0167-2681(82)90011-7

Harig, B. (2004, April 26). Woods "uncomfortable" with his game. *ESPN.* Retrieved from http://sports.espn.go.com/golf/news/story?id=1798899

Hemp, P., & Stewart, T. A. (2004). Leading change when business is good [Interview with Samuel J. Palmisano]. *Harvard Business Review 82*(12), 60–70.

Higgs, M., & Rowland, D. (2005). All changes great and small: Exploring approaches to change and its leadership. *Journal of Change Management 5*, 121–151. doi:10.1080/14697010500082902

Hoffman, E., McCabe, K. A., & Smith, V. L. (1996). On expectations and the monetary stakes in ultimatum games. *International Journal of Game Theory 25*, 289–301. doi:10.1007/BF0242 5259

Isern, J., & Pung, C. (2006). *Organizing for successful change management: A McKinsey global survey.* Retrieved from 7CGroup website: http://7cgroup.com/wp-content/uploads/2015/03/Organizing-for-successful-change-management.pdf

Kahneman, D., Slovic, P., & Tversky, A. (Eds.). (1982). *Judgment under heuristic: Heuristics and biases.* Cambridge: Cambridge University Press.

Kahneman, D., & Tversky, A. (1973). Availability: A heuristic of judging frequency and probability. *Psychological Review*, 207–232.

Kahneman, D., & Tversky, A. (1979). Prospect Theory: An analysis of Decision under Risk. *Econometica 47*(2), 263–292.

Kahneman, D., & Tversky, A. (1984). Choices, values, and frames. *American Psychologist 39*, 341–350. doi:10.1037/0003-066X.39.4.341

Keller, S., & Price, C. (2011). *Beyond performance: How great organizations build ultimate competitive advantage.* San Francisco: Wiley.

Kotter, J. (1995, March–April). Leading change: Why transformation efforts fail. *Harvard Business Review*, 59–67.

Kotter, J. P., & Heskett, J. L. (1992). *Corporate culture and performance.* New York, NY: Free Press.

Langer, E. J. (1982). The illusion of control. In D. Kahneman, P. Slovic, & A. Tversky (Eds.), *Judgment under uncertainty: Heuristics and biases* (pp. 231–238). Cambridge, UK: Cambridge University Press.

McKinsey & Company Organization Practice. (2013). *Building the leadership bench: building a talent pipeline for the senior executive services.* Washington, DC: Author.

Miller, D. (2002). Successful change in leaders: What makes them? What do they do that is different? *Journal of Change Management 2*, 359–368. doi:10.1080/714042515

Mohr, B. J., & Watkins, J. M. (2002). *The essentials of appreciative inquiry: A roadmap for creating positive futures.* Waltham, MA: Pegasus Communications.

Price, C., & Lawson, E. (2003). The psychology of change management. *The McKinsey Quarterly, Special Edition* (2), 30–41. Retrieved from http://www.mckinsey.com/insights/organization/the_psychology_of_change_management

Priestland, A., & Hanig, R. (2005). Development of first-level leaders. *Harvard Business Review 83*(6), 112–120.

Roberts, D. (2002). *Easy to do business with: The way ahead for PFS.* London: Barclays.

Ross, M., & Sicoly, F. (1979). Egocentric biases and availability and attribution. *Journal of Personality and Social Psychology 37*, 322–336. doi:10.1037/0022-3514.37.3.322

Sanfey, A. G., Rilling, J. K., Aronson, J. A., Nystrom, L. E., & Cohen, J. D. (2003). The neural bias of economic decision-making in the ultimatum game. *Science 300*, 1755–1758. doi:10.1126/science.1082976

Schwarz, N. (1987). *Stimmung als Information: Untersuchungen zum Einfluss von Stimmungen auf die Bewertung des eigenen Lebens* (Mood rather than information: Studies on the influence of mood on the evaluation of one's life). New York, NY: Springer.

Sinclair, U. (1935). *I, candidate for governor, and how I got licked*. New York, NY: Farrar & Rinehart.

Svenson, O. (1981). Are we all less risky and more skillful than our fellow drivers? *Acta Psychologica 47*, 143–148. doi:10.1016/0001-6918(81)90005-6

Thompson, C. (2008). Is the tipping point toast? *Fast Company*. Retrieved from http://www.fastcompany.com/641124/tipping-point-toast

Whitmore, J. (2004). *Coaching for Performance: Growing people, performance, and purpose*. London: Nicholas Brealey.

Whyte, D. (1996). *The heart aroused: Poetry and the preservation of the soul in corporate America*. New York, NY: Currency Doubleday.

Zohar, D. (1997). *Rewiring the corporate brain: Using the new science to rethink how we structure and lead organizations*. San Francisco, CA: Berrett-Koehler.

3

FROM PERPETUATION TO INNOVATION

*Breaking through Barriers to Change
in Higher Education*

JONATHAN S. GAGLIARDI

ABSTRACT

A reinvention and realignment of higher education is in order, but
doing so requires a deep understanding of the challenges that have
stood in the way of continuously improving student outcomes and
closing equity gaps, as well as the arrangements of public institutions and systems. This chapter explores past efforts at improving postsecondary access, as well as modern system-led efforts at
improving student outcomes.

Fifty years ago, the expansion of access to postsecondary education led to a period of social innovation within public U.S. colleges and universities. While efforts to increase access were largely
successful in terms of diversifying the student body, they fell short
of ensuring equitable access and, most crucially, equitable outcomes
for all students. Today, it appears that we are on the verge of a new
era of transformation, focusing on improving student outcomes and
closing equity gaps. This development is timely, as external pressures related to student success and costs, as well as institutional
accountability, budgets, and finances, continue to rise. Meanwhile,

calls for tighter connections between the higher education community, the government, the private sector, and civil society are growing. Internally, administrators and faculty members continue to seek policies and practices that improve attainment, reduce costs, and alleviate fiscal pressures brought about by years of diminished or stagnant state and federal funding. Simultaneously, incoming students are bearing a higher cost burden when the risks associated with not completing are higher than ever before.

Given ongoing social, political, and economic changes, the need for a new era of transformation was foreseeable. The social and demographic diversity that budded decades ago is blooming; by 2043, it is expected that the United States will become a minority-majority country (U.S. Census Bureau, 2012). Our economic model no longer depends on material goods; instead, our most precious commodities are now knowledge and data, both of which are growing voluminously. People live longer; the dynamics of the home and workplace have changed; and technology has forever altered the size of our world, breaking down the walls of time and space within the span of a few generations. The world is constantly changing, and the U.S. public higher education ecosystem is no different (Levy & Merry, 1986; Martinez & Smith, 2013). When confronted with fluid environments in the past, our system of higher education has been recognized as a case study of innovation and entrepreneurship (Drucker, 1988). However, the ability of our system of higher education to transform again has been cast in doubt.

Despite constant change and perpetual external social, political, and economic pressures, our university systems still appear much as they did during a period of unprecedented growth in the 1960s (Berdahl, 1971; Carayannis & Campbell, 2014; Etzkowitz & Leydesdorff, 2000; Lee & Bowen, 1971; Lyall, 2013; Millet, 1984). Systems have encountered difficulties in moving beyond their traditional roles, including coordinating campuses, allocating resources, and developing policies, while also exploring ways to provide centralized services and efficiencies (Gerth, 2010; Martinez & Smith, 2013). This challenge can be explained, in part, by dynamics between systems and campuses that make change more complicated. Context matters, and in some ways the divergent histories, functions, and arrangements of systems and campuses can be impediments to successful transformation. Namely, these dynamics complicate efforts to bridge misalignments between what our public systems of higher education are—and what we need them to be (Lane, 2012; McGuiness, 1991).

The slow rate of transformation among our systems of higher education has implications for completion rates, which are stagnant or falling (Advisory Committee on Student Financial Assistance, 2012). The failure of students to graduate from college is especially problematic at a time when our society has recognized that greater levels of educational attainment are needed to preserve social mobility and economic competitiveness.

Context matters, and in some ways the divergent histories, functions, and arrangements of systems and campuses can be impediments to successful transformation.

As such, college completion is a social problem that our systems are trying to solve contextually, by taking into account the unique challenges that have emerged over time and will become more prominent in the future. They are doing so by embracing new roles and partnerships to navigate beyond barriers to success (Lyall, 2013; Millet, 1984). Some of these new roles for systems include (a) providing shared services, (b) setting system-wide goals and targets for student success, (c) offering solutions that can be customized for institutions based on their traits, (d) leveraging the power of the convening, and (e) creating economies of scale and scope through collective action (Gagliardi, Martin, Wise, & Blaich, 2015; King, 2013; Lane, 2012; Lane & Johnstone, 2013; Lyall, 2013).

A period of innovation that moves beyond access to increase completion is dawning. Ensuring its success requires a deeper understanding of social innovations and their implications for systems and their leaders. Such an understanding requires answers to questions, including: Why do innovations succeed or fail? What are intended and unintended consequences of innovations? How do you ensure that innovations become sustainable? How does this apply to previous efforts within the higher education community to improve student outcomes and close equity gaps? How might we consider the design of future efforts with the same aim?

To these ends, the purpose of this chapter is to examine, as a type of social innovation, system-led efforts at improving student outcomes. The chapter begins with a review of the literature on innovation and social innovation. It then describes the phases and key elements to successful and unsuccessful social innovations. The access agenda is then framed as a form of social innovation. As part of that framing, special attention is paid to misaligned social innovations that were designed to promote access and the evolving need to focus on completion and closing equity gaps. Examples of system-led efforts that are evidence-based and show the potential for impact are then detailed. Finally, key themes and implications are discussed.

INNOVATION AND SOCIAL INNOVATION

While innovation is an ambiguous phenomenon, definitions of it include introducing something new or different, making changes, and adding value (O'Sullivan & Dooley, 2009; Quinn, 1985). Innovation is complex; it requires the integration of a diverse set of variables and processes and can occur instantaneously or incrementally, as well as intentionally or organically (Kanter, 1985/2000; Martinez & Smith, 2013; O'Sullivan & Dooley, 2009). It involves creativity, purpose, and mindful and deliberate design, which are contextualized to provide value to organizations and people (Drucker, 1988; Kanter, 1985/2000; Rosenfeld & Servo, 1991). Diffusion and adoption are signs that an innovation has been successful, as it has created a new standard for doing things (Schumpeter, 1934/2000). Innovation is also cyclical and reaches its fullest potential when advanced in a continuous fashion. If innovation is not approached in this manner, it can become stagnant, which can lead to negative consequences that eclipse the value that the innovation was designed to create. Eventually, these unintended consequences can be perpetuated, which eventually begets the need for additional, more difficult, and dramatic change (Rogers, 2003).

The study of innovation and perpetuation is one of contrasts, despite their cyclical and related natures. Each requires different organizational arrangements and leadership styles. Innovation requires cultivation, whereas perpetuation benefits from conservation (Hanan, 1976; Kanter, 1985/2000; Stevenson & Gumpert,

1985). The source of innovation is often unpredictable, and defining success can be a painstaking and inaccurate process, making it hard to know how to monitor and track progress. The development process can be costly, and the returns take a long time to materialize (Biggadike, 1979; Quinn, 1979, 1985). Innovations can produce large volumes of knowledge that are difficult to chronicle and diffuse effectively, which can prevent an innovation's full potential from being realized. It can also lead to an innovation's stagnating, which may also result in deeply entrenched structures, cultures, and arrangements. Stagnation can make change efforts increasingly difficult and complex. Innovations that anticipate and overcome these challenges, however, often benefit from an environment that is flexible and interconnected. They also have committed leadership and diverse revenue streams. Successful innovations are often designed as a solution to a specific social challenge (Kanter, 1985/2000), as is evidenced by the increasing popularity of social innovation, which emphasizes solutions to shared problems and positive social impact (Fifka & Idowu, 2013; Phills, Deiglmeier, & Miller, 2008).

IMPORTANCE OF ADOPTION AND SCALING TO SUCCESSFUL SOCIAL INNOVATIONS

Osburg and Schmidpeter (2013) suggest that innovations of all kinds require time and maturation. Their lifecycle model includes various stages that rely on different skills, infrastructure, and resources. Santos, Salvado, Lopo de Carvalho, and Schulte (2013) point to the identification of a problem and the development of a solution as a critical first step. Through a process of trial and error and refinement and revision, sustainable and replicable models can be created. Subsequently, the development of a business model is of priority, as is growth management. Once proof-of-concept has been achieved, it can be diffused to various stakeholders and actors who can contribute to systematizing change (Mulgan, 2007; Santos et al., 2013). Models that describe this process vary in the number of stages and evolution points that they include, but each model focuses on the cycle of creating the solution rather than the cycle of implementing the solution (Baron & Shane, 2005; Kuratko & Hodgetts, 2003; Osburg & Schmidpeter, 2013; Sahlman, Stevenson, Roberts, & Bhide, 1999; Santos et al., 2013; Timmons & Spinelli, 2004).

For social innovations specifically, developing a solution with a complementary implementation plan helps to maximize the impact they have on society (Osburg & Schmidpeter, 2013; Santos et al., 2013). There are five life cycle stages to social innovations: idea creation, experimentation, organization, systematizing and scaling, and sustainability (Elkington, Hartigan, & Litovsky, 2010; Mulgan, 2010). See Table 3.1 for a list and description of the key phases of social innovations, in addition to questions for consideration during their design.

IMPORTANCE OF INNOVATION FAILURES AND STAKEHOLDER-CENTERED DESIGN

Innovation failures occur when design elements are not end user focused, communication is sparse and not tailored, stakeholders are not engaged throughout the process, continuous improvement is not pursued, and successful organizational routines are abandoned rather than simultaneously strengthened (Rogers, 2003). Further, social innovations often fall short of expectations for various reasons, including cost; not being effective enough; externalities, or costs or benefits that affect a population that did not choose to incur said cost or benefit; and inaction by people or organizations in a position to create change, which can occur due to both a lack of incentives to act and an insufficient voice to be heard (Rogers, 2003). Despite negative connotations associated with failure, many successful innovations begin as such (Seelos & Mair, 2012). It is important to recognize that the real value of innovation comes incrementally and through continuous learning; there is no silver bullet. By learning from failures, successful innovation becomes more likely.

Learning from failures also involves stakeholder engagement and communication, which should be primary drivers of the design process (Bhattacharya, 2013; Crabtree, 2012). Engaging multiple stakeholders throughout each of the phases of an innovation creates

Table 3.1. Phases of Innovation

Phase	Description	Key Questions
Ideation	• The point of ideation that comes from identifying a problem and finding a solution; the moment of opportunity recognition.	• What is/are the problem(s)? • What is/are the solution(s)? • How do they connect? • Who do they impact? • What are the externalities?
Experimentation	• The process of hypothesizing, information gathering, and initial experimentation. This could be considered a beta-test phase.	• Is there evidence of impact? • How did early adoption efforts succeed? Why? • Where did they fall short? Why? • Who are the experts at implementing this?
Organizing	• Reinventing and refining based on learnings from previous experiments. At this stage, a proof-of-concept is ready to be used to generate stakeholder buy-in and investment.	• Who will be part of the initial cohort? • Is there evidence of commitment and passion? • What investments will be or have stakeholders made? • Within and across systems, who are peers? Who have the same contexts (traits, demands, characteristics, and strengths)? How do you connect them?
Systematizing and scaling	• Developing an ecosystem of change agents who advocate the enactment of your innovation. Cultivating a critical mass who begins to change what is considered to be the norm. Developing networks, cataloging how end users have tailored the innovation to suit their context.	• Of the first cohort, where are the bright spots? • Who did this well? • How would they describe success? • Will they serve as teachers and diffusers of the lessons learned? • What tools were developed? • What obstacles arose?
Sustainability and new innovation	• Reaching the point of scale and adoption, where the innovation has now become the standard and complementary cycles of innovation begin anew.	• How do you ensure adoption? • What will make this sustainable? • How will this be communicated, diffused, and replicated? • Who will be a part of the second cohort? • How can you continue to innovate through refinement and revision of this process?

Note: Adapted from Mulgan (2007).

ownership and buy-in, as well as insight, if done properly. "In sum, if one follows a stakeholder-centric approach, there are four steps to successfully generating social innovation ideas: articulating unmet social needs, generating ideas to meet those needs, distilling ideas, and selecting ideas to pursue" (Bhattacharya, 2013, p. 149). This approach hinges on effective, contextualized, and customized communication, which can help combat entrenched attitudes, behaviors, and cultures (Mulgan, 2007). It can be enhanced through evidence and a data-informed approach, which together create a wealth of information to drive continuous improvement and effective collaboration (Bhattacharya, 2013; Guenther & Guenther, 2013; Rogers, 2003; Zimpher, 2013).

CONSEQUENCES FOR MORE SUSTAINABLE SOLUTIONS

In many ways, expanding access to higher education is a case study of the intended and unintended consequences of social innovations.

How well one manages to engage, communicate, and co-develop an innovation with stakeholders has implications for its effects. The consequences of an innovation can be categorized in three ways: desirable versus undesirable, direct versus indirect, and anticipated versus unanticipated (Rogers, 2003). Depending on the nature of the consequences, further reinventions will be required, hence the importance of continuous improvement. According to Rogers (2003), if special attention is not paid to stakeholder-centered design, socioeconomic gaps widen because groups perched atop socioeconomic hierarchies are more likely to be early adopters. These groups enjoy information of higher quality and volume, stronger networks, and greater resources (Rogers, 2003). To the extent possible, successful social innovations attempt to accommodate this reality. Table 3.2 offers a review of some of the critical elements of successful social innovations. In many ways, expanding access to higher education is a case study of the intended and unintended consequences of social innovations.

Table 3.2. Critical Elements of Successful Social Innovations

What?	Key Questions
Understand the value added and life cycle of innovation	• What is the value added society? • What makes this process or product novel? • How long will it take to see return on investment? • Will this occur after the implementation life cycle?
Establishing central control and transitioning to autonomy	• How do you start with central control? • What elements are nonnegotiable? • How do you transition to greater autonomy? • What flexibility will be needed, and when?
Progressively and continuously forming coalitions	• What relationships need to be formulated? • What is the correct volume of participants? • When do these need to be developed? • Who will aid in their development?
Developing new devices and solutions to embed change	• Do new roles need to be created? • Are there new rules, policies, and devices that are necessary?
Dissolving boundaries and brokering a dialogue between stakeholders	• How do these stakeholders interact? • How can other efforts and stakeholders amplify this? • What are our individual and shared responsibilities?
Cultivating evolutionary and revolutionary leadership	• Is there sufficient follow-through at leadership levels across the initiative? • How will leadership gather and connect people? • Can leadership see connections, envision new ideas, and chart a future course?
Reinventing innovations in customized and improved ways	• How can you help organizations adopt innovations in customized ways? • What systems do you have in place to monitor and track progress as it occurs? • Are you communicating reinventions contextually to adopters?
Understanding the consequences	• What are the possible: Desirable and undesirable consequences? Direct and indirect consequences? Anticipated and unanticipated consequences? • How are you planning to mitigate negative consequences? • What social innovations will be needed to overcome new problems?

Note: Adapted from Rogers (2003) and Santos et al. (2013).

SOCIAL INNOVATION IN HIGHER EDUCATION: EXPANDING ACCESS BY IMPROVING STUDENT OUTCOMES

One of the preeminent social problems faced by the United States in the 1940s was a need for a more highly educated citizenry. There were concerns that returning soldiers would struggle with their transition to civilian life, from both social and economic perspectives. Uncertainty surrounding national security was on the rise due in part to advances in weaponry. A looming Cold War magnified international tensions and competition, particularly with the USSR. At that time, our collective consciousness was drifting toward the Space Race. However, the most important race was not occurring outside of our atmosphere; it was happening in our classrooms and our lecture halls. Facing serious deficits in educational attainment, Bush (1945) wrote:

> Higher education in this country is largely for those who have the means. . . . There are talented individuals in every segment of the population, but with few exceptions those without the means of buying higher education go without it. Here is a tremendous waste of the greatest resource of a nation—the intelligence of its citizens. (p. 25)

The President's Commission on Higher Education (1947) further highlighted the need for social mobility and economic growth by elaborating on challenges that included access barriers, economic barriers, restricted curriculum, and racial and religious barriers. At the same time that this social problem was emerging, a series of policy and organizational innovations were designed to solve it. Policies such as the Servicemen's Readjustment Act of 1944 (commonly known as the GI Bill) and the Higher Education Act of 1965 were created to promote a shift in higher education access from the elite to the masses. Further, a series of organizational innovations occurred with the same goals in mind (Brint & Karabel, 1989; Lee & Bowen, 1971).[1] This included the development[2] of community colleges;[3] an increase in the number of public universities; and the emergence of higher education systems, coordinating boards, and multicampus universities (Brint & Karabel, 1989; Lee & Bowen, 1971). These policies and structures, each aimed at expanding access and opportunity, were social innovations and helped frame higher education as a public good. To a degree, these social innovations were successful. Indeed, Figure 3.1 illustrates the rapid growth in educational attainment by the 25-and-older population between 1940 and 2013.

While the mass expansion of higher education has been a successful social innovation, unintended consequences have emerged, particularly as enrollment demographics have changed. Over the last 30 years, we have seen a growing education deficit that has weakened our national economic competitiveness and has threatened to reverse gains in social mobility. In global rankings, the

Figure 3.1. Years of School Completed by People 25 Years and Over: (Population in Thousands) Selected Years 1940 to 2012.

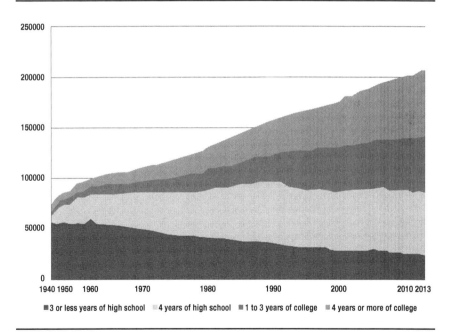

Source: US Census Bureau 1947, 1952–2002 March Current Population Survey, 2003–2014 Annual Social and Economic Supplement to the Current Population Survey; 1940–1960 Census of Population.

United States has fallen from first place in four-year degree attainment among 25- to 34-year-olds in 1990 to twelfth place in 2014 (OECD, 2013). Understanding why this drop has occurred is crucial to further improving the prospects of postsecondary completion for all students.

UNFORESEEN CONSEQUENCES OF PREVIOUS INNOVATIONS

Emphasizing Access and Working against Completion

As the number of campuses increased to meet the demands for increased access to postsecondary education, a complex web of horizontal and vertical structures were also put into place. These developments led to a loosely coupled system of higher education, and the missions and purposes of its constituent—separate but newly connected—organizations were vague (Cohen & March, 1986; Keeling, Underhile, & Wall, 2007; Lee & Bowen, 1971; Mintzberg, 1979; Weick, 1976). According to Keeling, Underhile, and Wall (2007), this approach was used to "allow for creative thinking, and to respect—and even encourage—the autonomy of different disciplines" (p. 1), which even then was in conflict with growing demands for assessment and accountability. Within this decentralized campus structure is a mixture of cultures across disciplinary and administrative units that have differing interests and goals. These differences can be barriers to broader institutional objectives focused on improving student outcomes (Clark, 1963/2000; Keeling, Underhile, & Wall, 2007; Schroeder, 1999).

The parallel development of postsecondary systems and coordinating boards added even greater complexity to the higher education landscape. These governance structures were designed to employ organizational techniques that were adopted from industry and government to centralize authority, consequently shifting some control away from campuses. Lee and Bowen (1971) allude to a "largely hidden battle . . . over how much less campus authority there would be" (p. xii.). As a result, natural tensions emerged between campuses and governance structures. Decentralized campuses and disciplines that were both academic and autonomous—

and which had developed over decades, if not longer—now were grappling with centralized and administrative governance structures that served as regulators, allocators, and coordinators (Lane, 2012). While these tensions have always been present, their unintended consequences have become more apparent as time has passed, and students and the demands placed on higher education have changed. These horizontal misalignments make an approach based on "systemness" difficult to realize, despite its apparent benefits (Zimpher, 2013). They can lead to inefficiencies and redundancies that are artifacts of less-connected social and higher education structures.

A CULTURE FOCUSED ON PERPETUATION RATHER THAN INNOVATION

In the post–World War II era, a culture was created that prioritized ideation rather than true innovation, which includes adoption, reinvention, customization, and sustainability. These policy and organizational innovations developed their own structures, functions, and fields, each of which had its own set of producers, consumers, and agencies, ultimately shaping higher education into what it is today (DiMaggio & Powell, 1983). According to Scott (2005), "the processes by which structures, including schemas, rules, norms, and routines, become established as authoritative guidelines for social behavior" (p. 2) serve as forms of oversight, by which actors in a given field are indoctrinated (Bourdieu, 1986; Lane, 2007; Scott, 2005). Structures serve to provide stability, but they are not changed easily, and efforts to do so can result in resistance.

Higher education is no stranger to this phenomenon. In addition to the internal tensions and resistance that arise between campuses and governance structures, tensions exist within campuses and among faculty members. The nature of faculty training and status leads many instructors to "cherish autonomy from direct control by administrative authorities" (Hearn, 2006, p. 5). Demands for research productivity have led to a separation between teaching and research (Brint, 2011; Rhoades, 2012). Reward systems encourage senior or tenure-track faculty to conduct research rather than focus on teaching (Rhoades, 2007, 2012; Smith & Rhoades, 2006). It is also suggested that faculty favor their disciplinary community instead of their campus community, making it more difficult to achieve the goals of the institution (Clark, 1963/2000; Kuh, 1996; Schroeder, 1999). This perspective can be detrimental to undergraduate students' graduation rates (Ehrenberg & Zhang, 2004). Bettinger and Long (2004) found that that substituting part-time faculty instructors for full-time faculty members decreases the likelihood that a student will continue taking classes in a subject. This approach to faculty staffing is untenable for emerging student populations that are increasingly diverse and transient.

In addition to the complex web of tensions that exist within campuses and between disciplines, as well as across campuses and their governance structures, external pressures also stem from the role of governance structures as boundary spanners. Over the last decade, stakeholders have developed alternative perceptions about the purpose, value, and function of higher education. This shift has created great turmoil, as traditional ways of doing things are coming under intense scrutiny at the hand of new agendas, purposes, and goals (Fligstein & McAdam, 2012; Scott, 2005, 2015). This change has disrupted the social, political, and economic capital around which higher education has traditionally been organized (Bourdieu, 1986). As conditions continue to change rapidly, the benefits of previous social innovations will diminish, while the effects of unintended consequences will be magnified (Rogers, 2003).

STAGNATING COMPLETION RATES AND WIDENING EQUITY GAPS

Although 66% of 2013 high school graduates enrolled in colleges and universities (Bureau of Labor Statistics, 2014), only approximately 59% of first-time, full-time undergraduate students who began their pursuit of a bachelor's degree at a four-year institution starting in 2006 graduated within six years (National Center for Education Statistics [NCES], 2014a), and just 31% of students seeking a certificate or degree at two-year degree-granting institutions completed a credential within 150% of normal time (NCES, 2014d). The apparent completion challenge becomes even clearer when data are disaggregated for underrepresented minorities and low-income students.

Of black and Hispanic first-time, full-time bachelor's degree-seeking students at four-year institutions, about 41% and 53%, respectively, graduated within six years after starting (NCES, 2014b). At two-year colleges, only 11% of black and 16% of Hispanic first-time, full-time students completed their credential within 150% of normal time (NCES, 2014c). Only 20% of Pell Grant recipients received a bachelor's degree, and approximately 25% attained an associate's degree or other credential (Pell Institute, 2011).

There are not enough people with a college credential—especially among underrepresented minority and low-income groups—for our country to remain economically competitive, and our system of higher education may be unable to achieve the ambitious goals set for it by myriad stakeholders (Lumina Foundation, 2013; White House, n.d.).

Equity Gaps May Worsen because Higher Education Is Not Set Up to Look Forward

Until recently, higher education has been retrospective rather than prospective, especially in the data that institutions collect and report and in the levels of analysis conducted across systems and campuses. Meanwhile, the higher education community has not defined analytics collectively in higher education, nor have we investigated its effects on the performance of higher education organizations (Foss, 2014). The data that we do have focus on singular institutions and specific populations that no longer compose the majority of students who enroll at higher education institutions. "Data analytics remains limited to the functional areas of admissions and enrollment management, business and finance, and student progression with little movement into the

There are not enough people with a college credential—especially among underrepresented minority and low-income groups—for our country to remain economically competitive, and our system of higher education may be unable to achieve the ambitious goals set for it by myriad stakeholders.

core academic functions of student learning, faculty productivity, cost to degree, and research administration" (Foss, 2013, p. 189). Data is topically stove-piped, further inhibiting the development of advanced progression analytics and cross-functional analyses that are crucial to improving student outcomes and organizational performance (Gagliardi & Wellman, 2014; Yeado, Haycock, Johnstone, & Chaplot, 2014). Further, the analytical functions at systems and campuses are drowning in a sea of demands (Gagliardi & Wellman, 2014; Gagliardi & Wellman, 2015). Consequently, the types of reports and analyses that are aligned with current and future challenges are of secondary priority to compliance reports that bear increasingly little value as demographics continue to change and resources stagnate. Both horizontal and vertical structures of higher education, as well as the data that we use to monitor and track progress, reflect past challenges and have not sufficiently evolved to meet future needs. Together, these misalignments may be contributing to deeper social inequality despite wholesale gains in educational attainment.

REALIGNING HIGHER EDUCATION TOWARD COMPLETION THROUGH SYSTEMS

Higher education systems are useful tools for encouraging colleges and universities to realign from a focus on student access to a focus on student completion. By providing shared services, setting system-wide priorities, driving innovation, and coordinating alternative pathways that include online learning, systems and campuses are leveraging one another in unprecedented ways (Mintz, 2014). The current emphasis on degrees has redistributed the responsibility of social mobility and economic growth more equally among research universities, comprehensive institutions, and community colleges. Due to their ability to serve as laboratories for innovation, hubs for analysis, and gatherers of organizational and environmental intelligence, systems are able to create economies of scale that are essential to meeting that shared responsibility, as well as current and future demands. Systems are increasingly important, and identifying examples of system-led innovations is critical to ensuring social mobility and economic growth. The following examples illustrate the vital role that systems play in innovating and scaling.

Problem: Remediation as a Huge Barrier to Completion
Solution: Redesigning the Math Pathway at SUNY

The State University of New York (SUNY) created the Task Force on Remediation in 2012. The charge of the task force was to investigate potential solutions, as well as implementation strategies, to decrease the need for remediation while simultaneously increasing the success rates of students who require it (SUNY Task Force on Remediation, 2012). The group's inquiry revealed that more than 40% of New York's high school graduates were college-ready. Further, more than 85% of black and Hispanic students graduated high school underprepared for college. Students requiring remediation were far less likely to persist than their college-ready peers, which is especially challenging at the community college level of SUNY, where most remediation occurs.

The task force identified several challenges, including a lack of adequate readiness assessments, the need for more targeted support for students requiring remediation, and insufficient funding mechanisms. Each of these challenges is further complicated by factors including "system-wide consistency vs. institutional autonomy, efficient vs. effective assessments of readiness, and supporting student progression and success while enforcing academic standards" (SUNY Task Force on Remediation, 2012, p. 8; see also Smith Jaggers & Hondra, 2011). Overcoming these challenges would be key to meeting the demands of a growing proportion of incoming students, while also driving down remediation costs and improving retention, persistence, and completion.

The task force identified the Quantway™ and Statway™ Learning Pathways, developed by the Carnegie Foundation and the Charles A. Dana Center at the University of Texas at Austin, as programs that could assist students who require remediation. The learning pathways were designed to help students in need of developmental math succeed in credit-bearing, college-level math and statistics courses. These programs help to shift learning mindsets, empowering students to believe in their ability to grow intellectually and improving their likelihood of success (SUNY Task Force on Remediation, 2012; Yaeger, Muhich, & Gray, 2011). There is promising evidence that the pathways are effective, "with 57% of students in Quantway™ completing their developmental math requirements in one semester, and 52% of Statway™ students receiving college credit in one year" (SUNY Task Force on Remediation, 2012, p. 19).

Seeing promise in these pathways with a proof of concept, two community colleges took the lead on a SUNY pilot, beginning by defining a mutual goal of dramatically increasing from 5% to 50% the percentage of students achieving college credit in math within one year of continuous enrollment. Since the initial pilot, many other community colleges across SUNY have expressed an interest in adopting the pathway models. Throughout the pilot, SUNY has deliberately left the decision to implement the Quantway™ and Statway™ models to math faculty at each of the campuses, in recognition of the critical role played by math faculty in testing, refining, and fully implementing new course pathways at the campus level. This approach avoided the perception that these pathways were simply a system-driven mandate. Further, these pathways have been designed with transferability in mind, not just within SUNY but outside of it as well. Despite still being a young initiative, the pathways are improving the progression of students who require remediation into college-level courses, while also better aligning diverse campuses to suit the needs of an evolving body of students.

Problem: Widening Equity Gaps in Higher Education
Solution: Predictive Analytics at the Tennessee Board of Regents

Access and attainment have increased for low-income, underrepresented minority and first-generation students since the 1960s but at a rate that is lower than that of the general student population (Denley, 2014). As a result, postsecondary attainment gaps have widened, threatening to undo hard-fought gains in social equity. This trend mirrors Rogers's (2003) warning that social innovations often have the unintended consequence of widening gaps, particularly when there are no efforts to engage and communicate with disadvantaged groups both in the design and diffusion of an innovation.

As part of their investigation into this challenge, the Tennessee Board of Regents (TBR) determined: "These attainment gaps appear to be significantly influenced by information gaps . . . without knowledge of the structure of higher education they [students who belong to low-income, underrepresented, and first-generation groups] are unable to even frame the questions that would enable them to become informed" (Denley, 2014, p. 61). This discovery represented the point of opportunity recognition for Tristan Denley, then the provost at Austin Peay State University (APSU).[4] After identifying information gaps as a problem, Denley and his team at APSU began developing a solution based on providing information to students in customized and intuitive ways. They harnessed principles of predictive analytics and behavioral economics and focused on "finding ways to empower student choices by creating choice architectures that improve the *information available to each student*" (Denley, 2014, p. 63; emphasis added).

This effort led to the creation of Degree Compass, a software program that leverages data on past student choices to anticipate likely student outcomes for each student as they consider taking specific coursework. During the experimentation phase at APSU, the software was connected to the institution's degree audit system, leading to the creation of an algorithm based on hundreds of thousands of student academic records. These aggregated data allowed APSU to make suggestions based on a student's likelihood of success in a course. The Degree Compass system also adds a star rating that is intended to represent courses that best fit a student's program of study and in which the student is likely to perform well. The design of Degree Compass mirrors popular streaming multimedia services, such as Pandora or Netflix, which offer suggestions for what media a specific person might like most. By creating a design intuitive to students, Degree Compass illustrates how intentional design can promote the success of an innovation (Denley, 2013). Integral to the experimentation stage was the creation of a robust assessment system that would allow for continuous refinement of the Degree Compass system. Eventually, further trials were run at three other institutions.

There was clear evidence of impact. Over 90% of students who took highly recommended courses received an A or B. The grades of students after the introduction of Degree Compass were 5 standard deviations higher than those of students prior to the implementation of the system (Denley, 2014). "This was especially true across the populations we hoped would benefit the most from better advice—African American Students (2.1%^) and Pell Grant recipients (3.9%^)" (Denley, 2014). Degree Compass also appears to have reduced the gap in earned credit hours between white and minority students. Preliminary evidence also suggests that attainment gaps have closed, albeit slightly. As a result of its effectiveness, $250,000 of nonrecurring funding was appropriated by the Tennessee legislature to facilitate statewide adoption of Degree Compass, which became effective on July 1, 2014. Efforts to scale across the TBR campuses have begun in earnest, as part of the Drive to 55 Alliance that is geared toward college completion (Baker, 2014).

Problem: STEM Degrees Unaligned with Workforce Demands
Solution: Scaling High-impact Practices at the California State University System

The demand for graduates with degrees in science, technology, engineering, and mathematics (STEM) disciplines has grown over the last few decades. Indeed, economic projections indicate that one million more STEM professionals will be needed if the United States is to remain competitive globally (President's Council of Advisors on Science and Technology, 2012). Determining ways to boost completion in STEM areas is crucial for economic reasons, and it poses a unique challenge to higher education. According to data from the National Center for Education Statistics (NCES, 2012), of 2003–2004 beginning bachelor's degree students, nearly half (48.3%) of students who majored in STEM left their major field. Students who were beginning associate's degree programs in STEM majors in 2003–2004 were even less likely to graduate; 36.5% of those students left higher education without a degree or credential. Further, black and Hispanic students and low-income students had the lowest chance of seeing their STEM degree programs through to completion. Credit accumulation in their STEM major and success in first-year college math courses were prominent reasons for their lack of persistence (NCES, 2012).

In recognition of this problem, the California State University System (CSU) has begun testing a model for "bringing high-impact practices ('HIPs') to more students" by following a successful model first developed at CSU Fullerton (Preparing to Scale High-impact Practices, 2014, p. 2; Taxonomies of High-impact Practices, 2014). The purpose of this project is to expand the diversity and scope of the STEM workforce pipeline. For this effort to be successful, challenges—including a lack of incentives and scaling and funding issues associated with HIPs—needed to be overcome. In response, CSU has launched several initiatives to improve learning, engagement, and persistence:

- Transforming course design: faculty development, specifically in high-enrollment courses with high levels of failure

- The graduation initiative: efforts to bring HIPs such as undergraduate research, service learning, and learning communities to the students who stand to benefit most from them

- STEM service learning: cross-sector collaborations aimed at developing experiential learning

- Early start: required enrollment in developmental education prior to the start of freshman year for low-performing students through summer bridge programs

During the experimentation phase, these initiatives were housed at specific institutions. For example, CSU Fullerton undertook efforts to assess HIPs and student participation, while CSU Northridge focused on summer bridge programs. Evidence of progress has taken different forms. CSU Fullerton is in the process of building the required infrastructure to be successful, including taking an inventory of HIPs; developing plans to scale up; creating a culture around HIPs through campus education, pilot programs, and developing methods of assessment (Bonsangue et al., 2013). At CSU Northridge, preliminary results suggest dramatic improvements in performance for students who participated in the Summer Bridge program versus those who opted out (Huber, 2010).

As evidence that supports these intervention strategies builds, CSU has been active in securing a more diversified funding base, including providing new system funding. In 2014, CSU received $4.6 million from the Helmsley Charitable Trust to create STEM collaboratives that aim to close achievement gaps in STEM fields for underrepresented and low-income students, in addition to creating standardized language and data that can promote continuous improvement and a better understanding of these interventions across the system and its campuses (CSU Garners $4.6 MIL Grant to Support Students in STEM Fields, 2014). To accomplish these goals effectively, CSU is experimenting at the individual campus level by organizing networks based on coalitions of willing campuses; promoting transparency, accountability, and learning within and across campuses; and continuously assessing to promote reinvention (Taxonomies of High-impact Practices, 2015; Relevant Findings, 2015). The steps undertaken represent a holistic approach to innovation that increases the likelihood of scaling, diffusion, and adoption across the entire system.

THEME: FOCUSING ON COLLECTIVE IMPACT FOR SUCCESSFUL INNOVATION

Misalignments that have developed over decades pose formidable challenges to shifting U.S. higher education's focus from access to completion. Given the growing importance of systems, system leaders play a critical role in creating sustainable social innovations that result in equitable student access and outcomes. For example, system leaders can begin to develop strong coalitions by working alongside campuses in crafting a unified vision based on common opportunities and challenges. System leaders are optimally positioned to engage with campuses, as well as bring campus leadership together to engage with one another. By serving as a convener and a networker, the system can make sustainable innovations that are driven by institutions. These functions help to overcome entrenched arrangements and resistance that commonly plague change efforts in higher education because they give campuses the opportunity of ownership of change efforts. This approach leads to a more comprehensive inventory of problems and potential solutions, in addition to the risks and rewards associated with each.

After working with campus leadership to define success and identify problems and prospective solutions, system leaders can use their capacity and central positioning to gather evidence and monitor progress in addition to serving as a hub for organizational intelligence. In the examples offered earlier, system leaders were effectively serving their campuses through intelligence gathering that could be customized to the unique characteristics and contexts of individual institutions.

Misalignments that have developed over decades pose formidable challenges to shifting U.S. higher education's focus from access to completion. Given the growing importance of systems, system leaders play a critical role in creating sustainable social innovations that result in equitable student access and outcomes.

By generating consensus around opportunities and challenges, and identifying potential solutions with a sound body of evidence, system leaders can also promote the effective organization of campuses that see value in adopting such innovations. It is important to take an approach that focuses on organizing a group of like-minded campuses that are ready to adopt an evidence-based approach, as it allows for early central control that can be quickly decentralized by working with coalitions of the willing. This strategy also negates the potential backlash that is possible if campuses perceive system action as an attempt to exert authority rather than as a resource. This progressive and continuous formation allows implementation to be devolved to the campuses that are willing to adopt the solution, without being too prescriptive. Again, in the examples discussed previously, successful system efforts identified campus champions and worked to ensure that they felt ownership over the process.

In each of these cases, systems developed networks among the adopting campuses, acting as a platform for coordination and information exchange, which helped to lower walls between distinct campuses. Systems that guided the organic development of communities surrounding specific innovations prompted greater collaboration and fostered dialogue between campuses. In some cases, to overcome barriers to sustainability, systems also worked to generate philanthropic and/or government funding to support the interventions for the longer term.

CONCLUSIONS AND IMPLICATIONS

The preceding discussion used the lenses of innovation and social innovation to explore how U.S. higher education institutions are innovating to shift from a student access agenda to a student completion agenda. As part of this presentation, a number of ongoing efforts to improve student outcomes were reviewed. The following conclusions, drawn from this review, may have implications for leaders of systems as they attempt to improve student outcomes and close equity gaps. Specifically, four transitions need to occur for U.S. higher education to successfully reinvent itself with a focus on student completion.

Transition 1: Rather than Perpetuate, Innovate

In direct response to growing national concerns, U.S. higher education reform efforts after World War II focused on expanding access and included the creation of policies and organizations that supported that effort. As such, they represented a social innovation, in that by expanding access to higher education, they promoted social mobility and economic growth for the entire country. Data suggest that policies and practices that promoted access to colleges and universities were largely successful in that they did increase access to postsecondary education. Now, however, these innovations require reinvention to accommodate the shift in emphasis toward student completion. As previously mentioned, reinvention and continuous innovation are a difficult state to achieve, particularly when they involve such a varied landscape of organizations and policies, each with their own cultures and arrangements and data that have over time shifted from innovating to perpetuating. What was good for access in the 1950s and 1960s appears to be misaligned to a great extent with what is needed for completion in the 21st century.

Transition 2: Move from Isolated to Integrated

By the time the need to shift from access to completion was identified as a social problem, the structures, arrangements, rewards, and behaviors of the myriad horizontal and vertical structures in higher education were entrenched. This situation led to isolated fields and organizations that were naturally in tension with one another. For decades, systems, campuses, and divisions acted in isolation, toward different ends, making it difficult for the goal of completion to take hold across systems and campuses. The function of time and entrenchment made such a shift more difficult for a variety of reasons. One of the unintended consequences of this culture of isolation was the widening of equity gaps, which has become more pronounced as the need for more interconnected campuses has risen due to changes in student demographics and enrollment patterns.

What was good for access in the 1950s and 1960s appears to be misaligned to a great extent with what is needed for completion in the twenty-first century.

Transition 3: Aggregation to Disaggregation

Broadening access and ongoing population changes—coupled with an increasing student cost burden, advances and technology, and more transient and diverse students—rapidly multiplied the contexts and challenges faced by incoming students. The development of equally disaggregated data and intervention strategies did not match the pace of change, however. Thus, one-size-fits-all solutions did not meet the needs of students, contributing to a widening of equity gaps despite wholesale increases in access and completions over the last half-century.

Transition 4: A Retrospective Approach to a Prospective One

Fundamental misalignments are reflected in how we monitor and track progress. Our current data infrastructure reflects a

System leaders can strengthen their efforts at innovation by leveraging their position as boundary spanners to unify institutions toward a shared goal based on data and evidence-based practices

homogeneous student population that has disappeared slowly over the last few decades. Such is evidenced by mandated compliance reports, including what is required for submission to the Integrated Postsecondary Data System (IPEDS), which still focuses on six-year graduation rates at one institution, and which fails to disaggregate student populations in ways that include low-income and underrepresented minority students. This problem is further reflected in the roles and functions of decision analytics and institutional research functions at systems, which remain topically stove-piped and still focus on transactional reports versus the strategic use of data. These functions are increasingly relied upon to respond to a sea of demands and compliance reports, while also conducting deeper predictive analytics. Despite this growing role, they lack the support and infrastructure needed to balance yesterday's compliance reports with matters more closely aligned with present and future demands on higher education, such as dramatic increases in completion. While these functions have attempted to migrate from explanatory to exploratory analyses that are more cross-functional, realistically they still have yet to jump from looking more closely into the past to peering into the future. There are a few examples of successful transitions, such as the examples previously discussed in the chapter, but there is still a long way to go if more customized, student-focused solutions are to be offered effectively with an eye toward completion and organizational effectiveness.

System leaders can strengthen their efforts at innovation by leveraging their position as boundary spanners to unify institutions toward a shared goal based on data and evidence-based practices. By further customizing and continuously improving these efforts, system leaders can create advantageous partnerships among the campuses they serve. Shifting the way data are used from a transactional model toward one that is more strategic can help system leaders allocate resources to the issues that matter most. Changing the approach to student success from one that is aggregated to disaggregated can help in creating programs and services that are designed with the varied challenges of diverse students in mind. System leaders can empower and support cohorts of campuses that are ready and willing to be more integrated by offering tools, data, incentives, and expert and technical assistance, where possible. Additionally, system leaders can help create meaningful change by focusing on the key phases of innovation, which go beyond opportunity recognition, and which entail experimentation, organization, scaling, and sustainability. By doing so, they can avoid stagnation, which over time can make improvement a daunting task. The cases presented here represent efforts undertaken by systems to do just that, and the subsequent conclusions and transitions observed are a means to bridge theory and practice and are designed to help guide system leaders as they innovate in ways that promote equitable access and outcomes.

NOTES

1. The Carnegie Commission (1967–1973) offered suggestions for a hierarchical system of higher education that pursued both quality and equality (Brint & Karabel, 1989, p. 104).
2. According to Lee and Bowen (1971), between 1958–1959 and 1968–1969, the number of governing and coordinating boards grew from 164 to 198 (+34). In that same timeframe, the number of systems grew from 63 to 84 (+21). In total, the number of public universities, four-year colleges, and two-year colleges was 855 in 1968.
3. Within 30 years of the community college boom, these schools would constitute over 40% of all undergraduate enrollments and over half of all entering students (Brint & Karabel, 1989, p. 103).
4. Denley now serves as the chief academic officer at the TBR.

REFERENCES

Advisory Committee on Student Financial Assistance. (2012). Pathways to success: Integrating learning with life and work to

increase national college completion. Retrieved from http://
www2.ed.gov/about/bdscomm/list/acsfa/ptsreport2.pdf

Baker, J. (2014). *A trailblazing promise*. Retrieved from http://www.
brightspace.com/blog/trailblazing-promise/#.VVFG8flVhBc.

Baron, R. A., & Shane, S. (2005). *Entrepreneurship: A process
perspective*. Mason, OH: Thomson/South-Western.

Berdahl, R. O. (1971). *Statewide coordination of higher education*.
Washington, DC: American Council on Education.

Bettinger, E., & Long, B. T. (2004). *Do college instructors matter?
The effects of adjuncts and graduate assistants on students'
interests and success* (National Bureau of Economic Research
Working Paper No. 10370). Retrieved from http://www.nber.
org/papers/w10370

Bhattacharya, C. B. (2013). The importance of marketing for social
innovation. In T. Osburg & R. Schmidpeter (Eds.), *Social innovation: Solutions for a sustainable future* (pp. 147–154). New
York, NY: Springer.

Biggadike, R. (1979). The risky business of diversification. *Harvard
Business Review 57*(3), 103–111.

Bonsangue, M., Cadwakkaderolsker, T., Fernandez-Weston, C.,
Filowitz, M., Hershey, J., Moon, H. S., Renne, C., Sullivan,
E., Walker, S., Woods, R., & Engelke, N. (2013). The effect
of supplemental instruction on transfer student success in
first semester calculus. *Learning Assistance Review 18*(1), 61–
74.

Bourdieu, P. (1986). The forms of capital. In J. G. Richardson
(Ed.), *Handbook of theory and research for the sociology of
education* (pp. 242–258). New York, NY: Greenwood Press.

Brint, S. S. (2011). Focus on the classroom: Movements to reform
college teaching, 1980–2008. In J. C. Hermanowicz (Ed.), *The
American academic profession: Transformation in contemporary higher education* (pp. 44–91). Baltimore, MD: Johns Hop-
kins University Press.

Brint, S. S., & Karabel, J. (1989). *The diverted dream: Community
colleges and the promise of educational opportunity in America,
1900–1985*. New York, NY: Oxford University Press.

Bureau of Labor Statistics. (2014). College enrollment and work
activity of 2013 high school graduates [Press release]. Retrieved
from http://www.bls.gov/news.release/hsgec.nr0.htm

Bush, V. (1945). *Science, the endless frontier: A report to the president.* Washington, DC: US Government Printing Office.

Carayannis, E. G., & Campbell, D. F. J. (2014). Developed democracies versus emerging autocracies: Arts, democracy, and innovation in Quadruple Helix innovation systems. *Journal of Innovation and Entrepreneurship 3*(12). doi:10.1186/s13731-014-0012-2

Clark, B. R. 1963/2000. Faculty organization and authority. In M. C. Brown, II (Ed.), *Organization and governance in higher education* (5th ed., pp. 119–127). Boston, MA: Pearson Custom.

Cohen, M. D., & March, J. G. (1986). *Leadership and ambiguity: The American college president.* Boston, MA: Harvard Business School Press.

Crabtree, J. (2012, September 12). Visionary tactics. *Financial Times.* Retrieved from http://www.ft.com/intl/cms/s/2/7d3afcde-fb0b-11e1-87ae-00144feabdc0.html#axzz3TX8fzv12

CSU garners $4.6 mil grant to support students in STEM fields. (March 17, 2014). Retrieved from http://blogs.calstate.edu/pa/news/?p=3893

Denley, T. (2013). *Looking to improve success.* Retrieved from Brightspace website: http://www.brightspace.com/blog/looking-improve-success/#.VPnB7vnF-2p

Denley, T. (2014). How predictive analytics and choice architecture can improve student success. *Research & Practice in Assessment 9*(Winter), 61–69. Retrieved from http://www.rpajournal.com/how-predictive-analytics-and-choice-architecture-can-improve-student-success/

DiMaggio, P. J., & Powell, W. (1983). The iron cage revisited: Institutional isomorphism and collective rationality in organizational fields. *American Sociological Review 48*, 147–160. doi:10.2307/2095101

Drucker, P. F. (1988). The coming of the new organization. *Harvard Business Review 66*(1), 3–11.

Ehrenberg, R. L., & Zhang, L. (2004). *Do tenured and non–tenure track faculty matter?* (National Bureau of Economic Research Working Paper No. 10695). Retrieved from http://www.nber.org/papers/w10695.pdf

Elkington, J., Hartigan, P., & Litovsky, A. (2010). From enterprise to ecosystem: Rebooting the scale debate. In P. N. Bloom & E.

Skloot (Eds.), *Scaling social impact: New thinking* (pp. 83–102). New York, NY: Palgrave Macmillan.

Etzkowitz, H., & Leydesdorff, L. (2000). The dynamics of innovation: From National Systems and "Mode 2" to a Triple Helix of university-industry-government relations. *Research Policy 29*, 109–123. doi:10.1016/S0048-7333(99)00055-4

Fifka, M. S., & Idowu, S. O. (2013). Sustainability and social innovation. In T. Osburg & R. Schmidpeter (Eds.), *Social innovation: Solutions for a sustainable future* (pp. 309–316). New York, NY: Springer.

Fligstein, N., & McAdam, D. (2012). *A theory of fields*. New York, NY: Oxford University Press.

Foss, L. H. (2014). *Integrating data analytics in higher education organizations: Improving organizational and student success*. In J. E. Lane (Ed.), *Building a smarter university: Big Data, innovation, and analytics* (pp. 187–211). Albany: State University of New York Press.

Gagliardi, J. S., Martin, R. R., Wise, K., & Blaich, C. (2015). The system effect: Scaling high-impact practices across campuses. *New Directions for Higher Education, 2015*, 15–26. doi:10.1002/he.20119

Gagliardi, J. S., & Wellman, J. (2014). *Meeting demands for improvements in public system institutional research: Progress report on the NASH project in IR*. Retrieved from National Association of System Heads website: http://www.nashonline.org/sites/default/files/initiatives/nash-ir-report.pdf

Gagliardi, J. S., & Wellman, J. (2015). Meeting demands for improvements in public system institutional research: Assessing and improving the institutional research function in public university systems. Retrieved from National Association of System Heads website: http://www.nashonline.org/sites/default/files/initiatives/improvements-public-system-institutional-research.pdf

Gerth, D. R. (2010). *The people's university: A history of the California State University*. Berkeley, CA: Berkeley Public Policy Press.

Guenther, E., & Guenther, T. (2013). Accounting for social innovations: Measuring the impact of an emerging intangible category. In T. Osburg & R. Schmidpeter (Eds.), *Social innovation: Solu-*

tions for a sustainable future (pp. 155–170). New York, NY: Springer.

Hanan, M. (1976). Venturing: Think small to stay strong. *Harvard Business Review 54*(3), 139–148.

Hearn, J. C. (2006). *Student success: What research suggests for policy and practice.* Retrieved from National Center for Education Statistics website: http://nces.ed.gov/npec/pdf/synth_Hearn.pdf

The Higher Education Act of 1965, 1 U.S.C. §§101–804 (1965).

Huber, Bettina J., (2010). *Does participation in multiple high-impact practices affect student success at Cal State Northridge? Some preliminary insights.* Retrieved from the California State University website: http://www.calstate.edu/engage/documents/csun-study-participation-in-multiple-high-impact-practices.pdf

Kanter, R. M. (1985/2000). When a thousand flowers bloom: Structural, collective, and social conditions for innovation in organization. In R. Swedberg (Ed.), *Entrepreneurship: The social science view* (pp. 167–209). New York, NY: Oxford University Press.

Keeling, R. P., Underhile, R., & Wall, A. F. (2007). Horizontal and vertical structures: The dynamics of organization in higher education. *Liberal Education 93*(4). Retrieved from http://www.aacu.org/publications-research/periodicals/horizontal-and-vertical-structures-dynamics-organization-higher

King, C. J. (2013). Board governance of public university systems: Balancing institutional independence and system coordination. In J. E. Lane & D. B. Johnstone (Eds.), *Higher education systems 3.0: Harnessing systemness, delivering performance* (pp. 149–168). Albany: State University of New York Press.

Kuh, G. D. (1996). Guiding principles of creating seamless learning environments for undergraduates. *Journal of College Student Development 37*(2), 135–148.

Kuratko, D. F., & Hodgetts, R. M. (2003). *Entrepreneurship: Theory, process, and practice.* Mason, OH: Thomson.

Lane, J. E. (2007). The spider web of oversight: An analysis of external oversight of higher education. *Journal of Higher Education 78*, 615–644. doi:10.1353/jhe.2007.0038

Lane, J. E. (2012). Higher education and economic competitiveness. In J. E. Lane & D. B. Johnstone (Eds.), *Universities and colleges as economic drivers: Measuring higher education's role in economic development* (pp. 1–30). Albany: State University of New York Press.

Lane, J. E., & Johnstone, D. B. (Eds.). (2013). *Higher education systems 3.0: Harnessing systemness, delivering performance.* Albany: State University of New York Press.

Lee, E. C., & Bowen, F. M. (1971). *The multicampus university: A study on academic governance.* New York, NY: McGraw-Hill.

Levy, A., & Merry, U. (1986). *Organizational transformation: Approaches, strategies, theories.* New York, NY: Praeger.

Lumina Foundation. (2013). *Goal 2025.* Retrieved from http://www.luminafoundation.org/goal_2025

Lyall, C. C. (2013). Reorganizing higher education systems: By drift or design? In J. E. Lane & D. B. Johnstone (Eds.), *Higher education systems 3.0: Harnessing systemness, delivering performance* (pp. 149–168). Albany: State University of New York Press.

Martinez, M., & Smith, B. (2013). Systems, ecosystems, and change in state-level public higher education. In J. E. Lane & D. B. Johnstone (Eds.), *Higher education systems 3.0: Harnessing systemness, delivering performance* (pp. 169–192). Albany: State University of New York Press.

McGuiness, A. C., Jr. (1991). *Perspective on the current status of and emerging issues for public multicampus higher education systems* (AGB Occasional Paper No. 3). Washington, DC: Association of Governing Boards of Colleges and Universities.

Millet, J. D. (1984). *Conflict in higher education: State government coordination versus institutional independence.* San Francisco, CA: Jossey-Bass.

Mintz, S. (2014, March 26). The shifting role of university systems. *Inside Higher Ed.* Retrieved from https://www.insidehighered.com/blogs/higher-ed-beta/shifting-role-university-systems

Mintzberg, H. (1979). *The structuring of organizations: A synthesis of the research.* Englewood Cliffs, NJ: Prentice-Hall.

Mulgan, G. (2007). *Social innovation: What it is, why it matters and how it can be accelerated.* Retrieved from Young Foundation website: http://youngfoundation.org/publications/social-innovation-what-it-is-why-it-matters-how-it-can-be-accelerated/

Mulgan, G. (2010). Measuring social value. *Stanford Social Innovation Review.* Retrieved from http://www.ssireview.org/articles/entry/measuring_social_value

National Center for Education Statistics. (2012). *STEM in postsecondary education: Entrance, attrition, and coursetaking among 2003–04 beginning postsecondary students.* Retrieved from http://nces.ed.gov/pubs2013/2013152.pdf

National Center for Education Statistics. (2014a). *Fast facts: Graduation rates.* Retrieved from http://nces.ed.gov/fastfacts/display. asp?id=40

National Center for Education Statistics. (2014b). *Graduation rate from first institution attended for first-time, full-time bachelor's degree-seeking students at 4-year postsecondary institutions, by race/ethnicity, time to completion, sex, control of institution, and acceptance rate: Selected cohort entry years, 1996 through 2007.* Retrieved from http://nces.ed.gov/programs/digest/d14/tables/dt14_326.10.asp

National Center for Education Statistics. (2014c). *Graduation rate from first institution attended within 150 percent of normal time for first-time, full-time degree/certificate-seeking students at 2-year postsecondary institutions, by race/ethnicity, sex, and control of institution: Selected cohort entry years, 2000 through 2010.* Retrieved from http://nces.ed.gov/programs/digest/d14/tables/dt14_326.20.asp?current=yes

National Center for Education Statistics. (2014d). *Institutional retention and graduation rates for undergraduate students.* Retrieved from http://nces.ed.gov/programs/coe/indicator_cva. asp

Organisation for Economic Co-operation and Development (OECD). (2013). *Education at a glance 2013: OECD Indicators.* Retrieved from http://www.oecd.org/edu/eag2013%20%28eng%29—FINAL%2020%20June%202013.pdf

Osburg, T., & Schmidpeter, R. (2013). *Social innovation: Solutions for a sustainable future.* New York, NY: Springer.

O'Sullivan, D., & Dooley, L. (2009). *Applying innovation.* Thousand Oaks, CA: Sage.

Pell Institute. (2011). *Pell Institute fact sheet: 6-year degree attainment rates for students enrolled in a post-secondary institution.* Retrieved from http://www.pellinstitute.org/downloads/fact_sheets-6-Year_DAR_for_Students_Post-Secondary_Institution_121411.pdf

Phills, J. A., Jr., Deiglmeier, K., & Miller, D. T. (2008). Rediscovering social innovation. *Stanford Social Innovation Review.*

Retrieved from http://www.ssireview.org/articles/entry/
rediscovering_social_innovation

Preparing to Scale High-impact Practices. (2014). Retrieved from
http://www.calstate.edu/engage/documents/Invitation-to-CSU-
Campuses-Preparing-to-Scale-HIPs.pdf

President's Commission on Higher Education. (1947). *Establishing the goals: Higher education for American democracy.*
Retrieved from Hathi Trust website: http://catalog.hathitrust.
org/Record/001117586

President's Council of Advisors on Science and Technology. (2012).
*Engage to excel: Producing one million additional college
graduate with degrees in science, technology, engineering, and
mathematics.* Retrieved from White House website: http://www.
whitehouse.gov/sites/default/files/microsites/ostp/pcast-execu-
tive-report-final_2-13-12.pdf

Quinn, J. B. (1979). Technological innovation, entrepreneurship,
and strategy. *Sloan Management Review 20*(3), 19–30.

Quinn, J. B. (1985). Managing innovation chaos. *Harvard Business
Review 63*(3), 73–84.

Relevant findings. (2015). Retrieved from the California State University website: http://www.calstate.edu/engage/findings/

Rhoades, G. (2007). Technology-enhanced courses and a mode
III organization of instructional work. *Tertiary Education and
Management 13*, 1–17. doi:10.1080/13583880601145496

Rhoades, G. (2012). *Faculty engagement to enhance student attainment.* Retrieved from American Council on Education website:
http://www.acenet.edu/news-room/Documents/Faculty-Engage-
ment-to-Enhance-Student-Attainment—Rhoades.pdf

Rogers, E. M. (2003). *Diffusion of innovations.* New York, NY:
Free Press.

Rosenfeld, R., & Servo, J. C. (1991). Facilitating innovation in
large organizations. In J. C. Henry & D. Walker (Eds.), *Managing innovation* (pp. 28–40). London, UK: Sage.

Sahlman, W. A., Stevenson, H. H., Roberts, M. J., & Bhide, A.
(Eds.). (1999). *The entrepreneurial venture* (2nd ed.). Cambridge, MA: Harvard Business School Press.

Santos, F., Salvado, J. C., Lopo de Carvalho, I., & Schulte, U. G.
(2013). The life cycle of social innovations. In T. Osburg & R.

Schmidpeter (Eds.), *Social innovation: Solutions for a sustainable future* (pp. 183–196). New York, NY: Springer.

Schroeder, C. C. 1999. Forging educational partnerships that advance student learning. In G. S. Blimling & E. J. Whitt (Eds.), *Good practice in student affairs: Principles to foster student learning* (pp. 133–156). San Francisco, CA: Jossey-Bass.

Schumpeter, J. A. (1934/2000). Entrepreneurship as innovation. In R. Swedberg (Ed.), *Entrepreneurship: The social science view* (pp. 51–75). New York, NY: Oxford University Press.

Scott, W. R. (2005). Institutional theory: Contributing to a theoretical research program. In K. G. Smith & M. A. Hitt (Eds.), *Great minds in management: The process of theory development* (pp. 460–484). Oxford, UK: Oxford University Press.

Scott, W. R. (2015). Education in America: Multiple field perspectives. In M. W. Kirst & M. L. Stevens, *Remaking college: The changing ecology of higher education* (pp. 19–38). Stanford, CA: Stanford University Press.

Seelos, C., & Mair, J. (2012). Innovation is not the Holy Grail. *Stanford Social Innovation Review*. Retrieved from http://www.ssireview.org/articles/entry/innovation_is_not_the_holy_grail

The Serviceman's Readjustment Act of 1944, 1 U.S.C. §§1767-24 (1944).

Smith, V. C., & Rhoades, G. (2006). Community college faculty and web-based classes. *Thought & Action, 22*. Retrieved from National Education Association website: http://www.nea.org/assets/img/PubThoughtAndAction/TAA_06_10.pdf

Smith Jaggers, S., & Hondra, M. (2011). *The opposing forces that shape developmental education: Assessment, placement, and progression at CUNY community colleges* (CCRC Working Paper No. 36). Retrieved from Teachers College, Columbia University website: http://ccrc.tc.columbia.edu/media/k2/attachments/opposing-forces-shape-developmental.pdf

Stevenson, H. H., & Gumpert, D. E. (1985). The heart of entrepreneurship. *Harvard Business Review 85*(2), 85–94.

SUNY Task Force on Remediation. (2012). *The SUNY pathway to success*. Retrieved from State University of New York website: http://blog.suny.edu/2013/01/2012-year-in-review-chancellors-task-force-on-remediation/

Taxonomies of High-impact Practices. (2015). Retrieved from the California State University website: http://www.calstate.edu/engage/taxonomies/index.shtml

Timmons, J. A., & Spinelli, S. (2004). *New venture creation: Entrepreneurship for the 21st century*. Boston, MA: McGraw-Hill.

U.S. Census Bureau. (2012). U.S. Census Bureau projections show a slower growing, older, more diverse nation a half century from now [Press release]. Retrieved from https://www.census.gov/newsroom/releases/archives/population/cb12-243.html

Weick, K. E. (1976). Education organizations as loosely coupled systems. *Administrative Science Quarterly 21*, 105–122. doi:10.2307/2391875

White House. (n.d.). *Higher education*. Retrieved from http://www.whitehouse.gov/issues/education/higher-education

Yeado, J., Haycock, K., Johnstone, R., & Chaplot, P. (2014). Education trust higher education practice guide: Learning from high-performing and fast-gaining institutions, top 10 analyses to provoke discussion and action on college completion. Retrieved from: http://edtrust.org/resource/education-trust-higher-education-practice-guide-learning-from-high-performing-and-fast-gaining-institutions/

Yeager, D., Muhich, J., & Gray, N. (2011). *What we're learning about productive persistence: Early evidence from the Statway*. Presentation at the Carnegie Foundation for the Advancement of Teaching's Winter Quantway Institute.

Zimpher, N. L. (2013). Systemness: Unpacking the value of higher education systems. In J. E. Lane & D. B. Johnstone (Eds.), *Higher education systems 3.0: Harnessing systemness, delivering performance* (pp. 27–44). Albany: State University of New York Press.

4

THE RISE OF COLLECTIVE IMPACT

JEFF EDMONDSON AND NANCY L. ZIMPHER

ABSTRACT

When the communities of Cincinnati and Northern Kentucky came together to collectively address the leaks in their educational pipeline, the successful process they used was not yet called "collective impact." This chapter discusses the development and struggles of the Strive Partnership, the emergence of the collective impact model, and the creation of a national network of communities working to improve educational opportunities for their children.

In 2006, a group of local leaders in Cincinnati came together for a town hall–style meeting to discuss a new college readiness program for low-income students. After much discussion, one of the participants, a county coroner, stood up and said, "As long as we remain program rich and system poor, we will not get more kids into college. And what's more, I'm going to continue to see dead kids on my table." The room resonated with the stark sense of truth and urgency in the statement. There it was. We weren't going to be able to program our way to better outcomes. We needed to find a new way of doing business.

This chapter originally appeared in the 2014 volume *Striving Together: Early Lessons in Achieving Collective Impact in Education*, by Jeff Edmondson and Nancy L. Zimpher, and is reprinted here with permission of the authors.

This pivotal meeting amplified the concern among many of us that focusing on college access was not enough—that, in order to truly move the needle on educational outcomes in the region, we needed to go much bigger by aiming for the *systemic* change needed to transform children's lives.

After more meetings with a growing and diverse collaborative of leaders, a new approach to social change was born. Beginning as a pilot partnership including three school districts in Cincinnati and Northern Kentucky, Strive set out to improve educational outcomes in the urban core of the region, not by starting new initiatives, but instead by scaling local practices that were already getting results for kids and building a stronger "civic infrastructure," which we have come to define as

> The way in which a region or community comes together to hold itself collectively accountable for implementing their own unique cradle to career vision, and organizes itself to identify what gets results for children; improves and builds upon those efforts over time; and invests the community's resources differently to increase impact. (Rospert, 2012)

Seven years later, Strive of Cincinnati and Northern Kentucky has measured remarkable results: The region has seen a 13-percentage-point shift in the number of outcomes trending positively, including a 9 percent increase in kindergarten readiness over four years across the three impacted cities of Cincinnati, Newport, and Covington. And today, Strive has given rise to StriveTogether, a growing national network of cradle-to-career partnerships across the United States.

... these leaders set out to improve educational outcomes in the urban core of the region, not by starting new initiatives but instead by scaling local practices ...

But that is truly the "long story short" of this full-length version of the Strive narrative. It needs to be said up front that we are true believers in this work. Having been involved since the very beginning, we have both seen the impact the Strive Framework can have on a community. Now, with the viral surge in replication of the Framework and its emerging Theory of Action, we decided the time was ripe to provide a detailed look at how Strive came to be. The desire to share success stories and lessons learned, warts and all, grows out of a fundamental commitment in this work to accountability, transparency, and continuous improvement. It also reflects our dedication to cultivate a strong community of practice, one that functions like a healthy ecosystem with effective feedback and adaptation mechanisms. This is not easily achieved, as will be made clear in these pages.

And this is also a story about quality, about the very real challenge of bringing discipline and rigor to the social sector. It's about acknowledging how hard it is to get people to work together who are often separated into silos. It is about using data consistently not as a hammer but as a flashlight to help us figure out how to make smarter investments. We have been riveted on bringing the discipline Jim Collins spoke about in his monograph *Good to Great and the Social Sectors*. "A culture of discipline," Collins (2005, p. 1) wrote, "is not a principle of business; it is a principle of greatness." And perhaps most important, it is about being willing to "fail forward": to make mistakes along the way, be transparent about what was learned, and make adjustments at the local and national levels.

A CINCINNATI STORY

Cincinnati is the third-largest city in Ohio, after Columbus and Cleveland. Its greater metro area, which expands in all directions, including southward over the Ohio River and into nearby Northern Kentucky, is home to more than 2.1 million people.

First settled in 1788, the city's location at the confluence of the Ohio and Licking rivers proved auspicious. As a convenient outpost supporting westward expansion, the settlement quickly built itself into the first major inland city in the United States, earning the nickname "Queen of the West," or the Queen City, as it is still often called. By 1880, it was the most densely populated city in the country, and the fast growth spawned the establishment of other cities nearby. Just over the river to the south, Newport, Kentucky, was settled in 1791, and Covington, on the west bank of the Licking, was established in 1814, close neighbors to Cincinnati that today are folded into the greater metropolitan area (Korte, 2008).

At the end of the 19th century, the region was a powerhouse of manufacturing and meatpacking and Cincinnati a boomtown churning with iron and cloth production and woodworking. There were also hospitals and opportunities for higher education, like the University of Cincinnati, which began as the Medical College of Ohio in 1819 (Ohio History Central, n.d.). The region had much to offer and for decades drew immigrants by the tens of thousands.

But like the rest of the country, Cincinnati's economic drivers changed over time; manufacturing, once the backbone of American money making, suffered and all but went away by comparison to what it once was. Still, today the greater Cincinnati area is home to several of what can be called strong anchor institutions, organizations that because of their size and deep roots in the community are not likely to pick up and move away, big businesses that are big employers. It is headquarters to nine Fortune 500 companies—household-name powerhouses like Procter & Gamble, Kroger, and Macy's, to name a few. The greater region is also home to many colleges and universities, as well as nearly 40 hospitals and, of course, beloved professional sports teams, the Bengals and the Reds.

But as the 20th century came to a close, while Cincinnati had many strengths and assets, there were also warning signs of significant challenges.

The Greater Cincinnati area reflected the national pattern of struggling urban education systems. Nearly half of Cincinnati Public School students were dropping out before graduating from high school (Cincinnati Public Schools, 2010). The numbers were equally concerning when it came to other indicators of the community's "education health": Kindergarten-readiness rates were below 50 percent, and reading and math scores, college enrollment, retention, and graduation rates were below state and national averages (Strive Partnership, 2008). Too many Cincinnati-area students were leaving high school unprepared for the workforce or college, an untenable trajectory for the local economy and quality of life.

These results were alarming not just for parents, teachers, and school administrators but were enough to catch the attention of the broader community. Like many cities in the United States, there was already a multitude of programs and services in place to help at-risk students. But then why were the numbers slipping or stagnating at dangerously low levels? A handful of Cincinnati-area leaders found themselves asking this question in earnest.

Then, months before the events of 9/11 shook the nation to its core, Cincinnati experienced its own painful entrance to the 21st century, with three days of violent and destructive riots in April 2001 triggered by the killing of a young black man by police. Cincinnati, a city known as a good place to live and raise kids, was left embarrassed and stunned after the riots, Dan Horn (2001) of the *Cincinnati Enquirer* later wrote. Not only was the city's outward image damaged; its sense of self was shaken. The riots of April 2001 forced Cincinnati and its neighbors to acknowledge that for all the good reasons to call the region home, there was a stew of deep-seated problems that were getting worse.

This combination of destructive events and frightening economic and educational indicators left the city with a sense of urgency, priming leaders to look for new ways of approaching problem solving . . .

This combination of destructive events and frightening economic and educational indicators left the city with a sense of urgency, priming leaders to look for new ways of approaching problem solving, an open stance that may have opened the door just enough to allow for the embrace of a very different approach to education reform.

A NEW KIND OF COLLABORATION

The work that ultimately evolved into the Strive Partnership was possible only through the participation of a wide range of leaders. Chad Wick, then president and CEO of the KnowledgeWorks Foundation (KWF), had been thinking for some time about how to improve the systems that drive educational outcomes. At KWF, Chad had been involved with the creation of the Cincinnati Youth Collaborative in 1986–1987 and had been involved in local education issues for more than two decades. In that time, he recalled seeing many well-meaning interventions and projects fail to improve high school graduation rates, specifically. Try as they might, the graduation rate dial was virtually unchanged from the early 1990s to 2001. "My DNA is to look for system solutions," Chad said, "and the beauty of KnowledgeWorks was that it gave me an opportunity to patiently look into these kinds of solutions and invest in those that would further education and youth development in a systematic way."[1]

Another key player was Kathy Merchant, president and CEO of the Greater Cincinnati Foundation (GCF). Kathy had long been tackling the city's quality of life and economic challenges with a group called Cincinnati Community Action Now (CAN), but she and her colleagues had yet to make a connection to education. According to Kathy,

> CAN worked for nearly two years after the 2001 riots to identify a range of initiatives that would improve the lives and the prospect of a brighter future for everyone in our community, especially poor families and disenfranchised African Americans. . . . Those initiatives spanned early childhood education, getting jobs for "hard to hire" persons with criminal records and other barriers, affordable housing, better access to health care, and of course improving police/community relations.

When CAN completed its work in 2003, the group created Better Together Cincinnati, a collaboration of funders who pooled over $7 million to support development of several new initiatives that CAN's leaders felt were missing in the package of solutions, including the Community Police Partnering Center and Minority Business Accelerator.

By 2005, those new initiatives were up and running, achieving small gains to advance the community's big goals. But, Kathy said, this was still not enough. "While acknowledging that reversing decades of lost opportunity would take a long time, and that GCF had chosen areas of focus wisely and well, we still felt that we were missing an important lever for change."

Chad's and Kathy's paths had been crossing regularly for many years, and the two had become close colleagues and friends. They saw the necessary connections to be made between schools and communities. They shared a desire to help Cincinnati's schools and communities make those connections, and they had many brainstorming sessions over lunch or dinner about how their own organizations could work together to help more kids succeed in and out of school. They knew that greater collaboration would benefit children, their families, and their communities, but they struggled with just how to take action.

In 2001, Rob Reifsnyder came to Cincinnati as president of the local United Way chapter. Chad and Kathy brought Rob into their discussions because they felt strongly that they would need a partner focused on providing youth services. Chad and Kathy quickly piqued Rob's interest, but the pivotal role his organization would eventually play in the development of the Strive Partnership could not yet be seen clearly. "I remember having dinner about this with Chad and Kathy," Rob said. He continued,

> They had me asking, "What does the map look like for our education system?" There are a thousand players, but nobody knows who's doing what to whom and why and when. I was able to see that there were a lot of entrepreneurial efforts springing up here and there, and many of them were doing great work, but it was really hard to know what the big picture looked like. United Way wanted to be a good supporting partner in this work, but we really didn't know where we could fit effectively.

Upon reflection, the Strive Partnership probably could not have happened without Rob's leadership in launching the United Way's Community Impact Agenda in 2003. It marked a critical transition from the United Way and its partners simply handing out grants to assessing how grantees moved specific outcomes. There was significant resistance in the community to using data in this way, but Rob persevered and helped leaders embrace more data-informed work.

Then, in 2003, Nancy was appointed to the presidency of the University of Cincinnati and arrived committed to the critical role of a university to engage deeply with its community.

She saw that a university's active engagement in the community was essential to that community's success, to creating good jobs and preparing people for those jobs, to raising the overall standard of living and quality of life. She knew that for the University of Cincinnati to reach its full potential, it needed the benefits of a thriving urban community. She also knew that being the head of a university meant more than being a campus administrator; it meant being a bridge to the community, reaching out and saying, "This university could help make this city the best place to live in America by asking: What can we do together to make that happen?"

Building a sustainable and successful Cincinnati, Nancy believed, would require higher education to forge strong links with P–12. This was something that Chad, Kathy, and Rob had not considered as they had been focused on making P–12 that primary driver. Nancy understood where higher education was falling short in its service to P–12, and vice versa, and where both could do better together. To really see high school graduation and college enrollment and completion levels rise, it was colleges and universities, not P–12 schools, that needed to get smart and serious about improving teacher training and working more closely with school systems to see that students were on track to be prepared for college. This meant cultivating relationships and forming partnerships. And it meant starting new conversations, which is what started happening in Cincinnati in 2003 when these leaders came together.

Based on her experience as the leader of a large, public urban research university in Milwaukee, and leading a network of similar institutions nationally, Nancy was ready to see UC merge its agenda with Cincinnati's future. She knew that future would be defined by our ability to educate better: a better college experience, better-prepared teachers to serve in our city's schools, and a better success rate for graduating high school students who are college and career ready. In the very early weeks and months as UC's new president, her calendar began to fill with meetings with the key people on campus and in the broader community who could make this vision a reality.

Chad had met Nancy years earlier, when she was dean at the College of Education at Ohio State University. But it was her work in Milwaukee that had really gotten Chad's attention. He saw that her approach sparked a new kind of university-community engagement that had far-reaching effects in the city, including the performance of its public schools. When he heard that she'd gotten the UC job, he dispatched a letter to her immediately, inviting her to meet him when she got to town.

The two met shortly after Nancy's arrival in Cincinnati and began to build the table that would become the initial Strive Partnership. "We were essentially soul mates, connecting on several levels," Chad recalled of those early conversations. "We were trying to create an atmosphere around public education of finding the common ground among schools, universities, and communities. We were trying to get everyone on the same page, and as president of UC, Nancy seemed to be elevating everybody to a higher plane."

The fall of 2003 was an intense series of reach-outs, connection-making, and meetings, as their table gradually expanded and more and more community leaders joined them in asking, "What can we do together to improve education outcomes in Cincinnati schools?"

While the discussions between Chad, Nancy, and a growing number of community leaders were steadily confirming the need for increased collective action, discussions in key K–12 sectors were anything but galvanizing. Meetings with the then–Cincinnati Public Schools superintendent started on a positive note, but he left the position before any action resulted from those discussions. His successor, who had been a deputy superintendent in the system but not part of those early discussions with the Partnership, initially closed the door to further dialogue, a position backed by the school board, which had appointed her with its own agenda and set of priorities. Not without reason, these district officials were suspicious of "help" from the outside. Far too often, partners come saying they want to work with school districts, only to try to impose their will down the road. As a result, district leaders felt distracted at best—burned at worst—by community partners who rarely respected their expertise.

Complicating the matter, the head of the teachers' union was engaged in bitter negotiations with the board and had sent a clear message that there was no place for this new partnership at their table.

This initial resistance in Cincinnati prompted Nancy and Chad to expand their reach into the neighboring school districts and higher education catchment areas. The idea was that if they could get these surrounding systems to sign on, Cincinnati would be more open to getting involved. The strategy worked. Growing cross-sector support became evident, and the Cincinnati Public Schools began to realize that they stood to benefit from the effort.

Former Covington Public Schools superintendent Lynda Jackson recalled,

> Originally, we thought we should get involved with the Strive Partnership because of money, and I think the district jumped on the train to follow the dollars. Then, as it evolved and things came to fruition, we realized it wasn't about the money. It was about thinking systematically about how we could build partnerships to improve student achievement in schools and work on the whole child, not just the academics, but also with community partners and parents and get everyone around the table.

Discussions with two area university presidents had quickly provided the added value Nancy and Chad needed. Father Michael Graham, president of nearby Xavier University, and Jim Votruba, president of Northern Kentucky University, located a short distance across the Ohio River, were also instrumental in the development of the Partnership. With the presidents of three major universities in the area vowing to develop a more coordinated approach to education from its earliest stages through college, P–12 support began to fall into place.

"We were concerned that too few students from our urban core were going on to college, and, if they did go on to college, too many were ill prepared to succeed," Jim recalled. He continued,

> Each of us understood that college readiness required more than a focus on the junior and senior year in high school. A more comprehensive approach was required to align the in-school and out-of-school development of children and to focus on the entire education continuum from early childhood through high school and beyond. What began as a college readiness conversation quickly became a conversation focused on comprehensive urban education

reform. I became involved in this initiative because I felt it provided the best opportunity to impact what I believe is the most important challenge confronting our nation. I continue to feel this way today.

Michael Graham echoed this sentiment:

Too often, we have tasked our schools to solve alone problems they are incapable of solving, problems whose origins in poverty and social change schools simply cannot solve alone. This kind of partnership enables a community to see how all of these issues exist on a continuum, understand what research tells us are the most effective levers for intervention at the crucial steps along the way, and muster integrated community support to enact change that works. As a priest, I grieve at the lost human lives our inaction creates. As a university president, I worry that not enough young people are adequately prepared for college. As a citizen, I fear that we are on the slippery slope of becoming a has-been, second-rate nation. Education is our future—individually and collectively—and this is a new way of addressing how we can get better results out of our educational systems.

This core group of top-level leaders from the region's three major universities, the school districts, and key social agencies and foundations later added the executives of several of the region's major employers and charitable foundations, leaders in early childhood education, and the directors of such civic groups as the Urban League. The Partnership ultimately became a broad and potent mix of leadership, skills, and influence, united by a broad common interest in improving education in the region.

The initial work consisted of significant outreach to the community as a whole. In addition to summarizing themes from years of engagement, community partners held a host of forums. In one gathering at Ninth Street Baptist Church in Covington, as one community member spoke highly of an after-school program she believed kept her child off the streets, another resident expressed anger and frustration that she was not aware of that program, that it was essentially left to chance as to whether her grandchild would be able to take advantage of the opportunity. And it became clear: With assets as precious as our children, we simply could not leave their future to chance.

Over the next four years, the conversation evolved, but the evolution was not always seamless or easy. We hope that the lessons learned in Cincinnati and Northern Kentucky, and the early experiences of other sites discussed here, can help other communities convene the necessary partners and seat them at the common table in a more timely and efficient manner.

A NEW WAY OF DOING BUSINESS

The community rallied around the concept that it was "program rich and system poor," but nobody had a clear path to determine what it meant to be "system rich." One thing was clear: Leaders from across sectors would need to work together, arm in arm, to develop a new way of doing business. Because this was not part of anyone's job description in particular, the Partnership would need, as Jim Votruba said, someone to wake up every day thinking about how to create this system by weaving together "what works" among the massive variety of programs and services in operation locally. It would take, the partners joked, something of a "cat-herder," someone with the problem-solving and task-management skills to bring together even the most complex set of professionals and programs.

Leaders from across sectors would need to work together, arm in arm, to develop a new way of doing business.

KWF loaned Jeff Edmondson to play this role and report directly to the community leaders at the partnership table and not to the KWF board. This decision gave Jeff increased credibility with the partners because it was their strategic direction he was tasked with carrying out, not KWF's or his own. Jeff listened to what the partners were interested in accomplishing together and formulated a strategy that kept them focused on their collective vision while meeting the "enlightened self-interests" of each partner. This way they could justify to their own boards why being involved in the Partnership contributed to their individual purpose.

The strengths and purposes of the different partners shaped the path of the work. Procter & Gamble helped lead a process to market the work. The districts were able to clarify what they really needed from the Partnership to help improve their bottom line: student achievement. And investors were able to identify the information and data they really needed to make more informed decisions. All of the partners embraced the concept of Robert Greenleaf's servant leadership without ever explicitly referencing it in the work:

> The servant-leader is servant first. It begins with the natural feeling that one wants to serve. Then conscious choice brings one to aspire to lead. The best test is: do those served grow as persons: do they, while being served, become healthier, wiser, freer, more autonomous, more likely themselves to become servants? And, what is the effect on the least privileged in society; will they benefit, or, at least, not be further deprived? (Greenleaf, 2002, p. 6)

With this approach to leadership as a foundation, the partners were willing to let KnowledgeWorks provide the staff to act as the "backbone," supporting a collective vision for the community as a whole. Their courage to lead in a new way made it possible for this work to come to life.

ARTICULATING A SHARED CRADLE-TO-CAREER VISION

The questions remained: Where do we start? Where should we begin to address the massive challenges confronting children in the region, especially those from poor families? What leadership roles might the various partners play to make sure the work is owned by the community, not a select few?

Given the critical mass of higher education leaders, the obvious first focus was college access and success, which fell squarely in the group's domain. Chad provided "backbone" staff at KWF to support the effort, under Jeff's supervision. Shortly thereafter, extended meetings were held at each of the three universities bringing together a diverse array of individuals committed to providing strategies and resources to make college access a reality for many more students, especially poor and minority youth support. At this stage, the effort was known as the College Access/Success Partnership (CAP).

By the summer of 2005, the CAP participants had formulated a vision and a mission for the Cincinnati and Northern Kentucky region; all students would have access to higher education and the opportunity to succeed in earning a degree. The education, philanthropic, civic, business, and nonprofit sectors would provide necessary academic and financial support by strategically aligning programs and initiatives throughout the region that promote college access and success. CAP's mission embraced three primary goals. First, CAP staff would coordinate existing college access and success efforts throughout the region by mapping their efforts. Next, they would align those efforts with the needs of postsecondary institutions, school districts, schools, and students and their families. And finally, they would monitor their implementations and measure their results.

While improved college access and success had now been defined as CAP's ultimate goal, it became clear as Jeff and his staff delved deeper into student data and an evaluation of existing programs that the region was "program rich and system poor." There were numerous programs that were serving youth with the goal of increasing college access and success locally, but taken together, they were not moving the collective dial. One of the core problems was not a lack of *effort* but a lack of *coordination*.

It was also clear that the obstacles standing in the way of college access and success among kids locally began much, much earlier than high school. Conditions surrounding children's lives both in and out of school—often before they were even school age—were at the core of the problem. This realization had the group circling back to the concept of the leaky education pipeline and their earlier focus on a wider effort that spanned that pipeline from cradle to career.

"The conversation became, 'Well, what is keeping kids from going to college anyway?'" Chad explained. "First we thought the problem was in high school, but then we realized it was elementary schools, and then finally, we said, 'this goes as far back as preschool.' And that is how it all began."

As their vision continued to take shape, partners began to pinpoint predictable and prevalent problems that confronted children at every stage of the pipeline and discussed interventions that could help children navigate those challenges and stay on the desired educational course. These discussions were the beginning of what later became the "Student Roadmap to Success" (figure 4.1), which was first sketched on a napkin at a local pub by a few key partners who were struggling to capture the new vision conveyed by their peers.

. . . the roadmap gives everyone involved in the process a complete mental picture of the work itself, beyond their individual scopes.

The roadmap was intended to be a visual depiction of the Partnership's ambitious goals for the region, serving students in school for the length of the pipeline but also providing more coordinated out-of-school supports beginning as early as a child's preschool years.

Nancy pulled together a UC team led by Larry Johnson, dean of the college of education and an outspoken advocate for youth, and his associate dean, Nelson Vincent, who worked with a cadre of talented doctoral students to develop the roadmap, a version of which StriveTogether still uses today. The roadmap went through several iterations before it was embraced by cross-sector leaders and began to be viewed as a guide for action late in 2005.

Asked to explain the importance of the roadmap, Chad said that one of its most valuable aspects is that the roadmap gives everyone involved in the process a complete mental picture of the work itself, beyond their individual scopes. "We come to this from so many different disciplines. We filter goals through our own mental processes, understandings, and emphasis," he explained. "The roadmap creates a mental model that causes everybody to suspend their view of the world and see the bigger picture. Because we all think in pictures, and the roadmap essentially gives us a picture of our interventions and what we are setting out to accomplish, it is a transformational tool."

Figure 4.1. Student Roadmap to Success

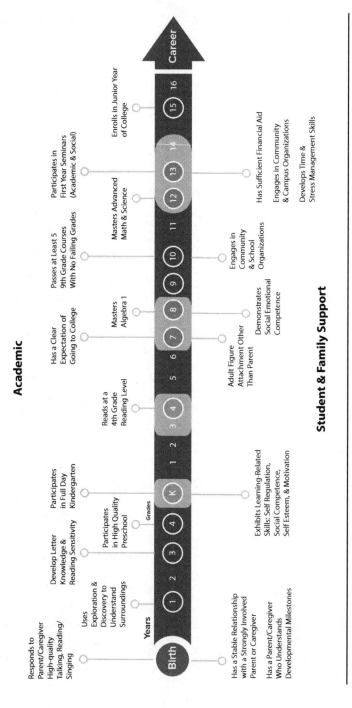

Academic

Responds to Parent/Caregiver High-quality Talking, Reading/ Singing

Develop Letter Knowledge & Reading Sensitivity

Participates in Full Day Kindergarten

Reads at a 4th Grade Reading Level

Has a Clear Expectation of Going to College

Passes at Least 5 9th Grade Courses With No Failing Grades

Participates in First Year Seminars (Academic & Social)

Enrolls in Junior Year of College

Uses Exploration & Discovery to Understand Surroundings

Participates in High Quality Preschool

Masters Algebra 1

Masters Advanced Math & Science

Years

Grades

Career

Student & Family Support

Has a Stable Relationship with a Strongly Involved Parent or Caregiver

Has a Parent/Caregiver Who Understands Developmental Milestones

Exhibits Learning-Related Skills: Self Regulation, Social Competence, Self Esteem, & Motivation

Adult Figure Attachment Other Than Parent

Demonstrates Social Emotional Competence

Engages in Community & School Organizations

Has Sufficient Financial Aid

Engages in Community & Campus Organizations

Develops Time & Stress Management Skills

Source: Courtesy of Jeff Edmondson and Nancy L. Zimpher

Going forward, we started every meeting with a display and reference to the roadmap, because of its compelling visual map of the journey from prenatal care and birth to career, and every important educational intervention along the way. It also kept the focus on academic assessments and improvement mechanisms (above the line) and critical social, family, and community supports (below the line) that ensure that children and youth arrive at school healthy, happy, and ready to learn.

THE WAY FORWARD: LAUNCHING THE STRIVE PARTNERSHIP

About three years into this dialogue, we got collective sign-on across Cincinnati and Northern Kentucky. The group's early focus on college access and success had provided an impetus for a broader vision, one that is depicted by the roadmap and underscored by the continuing leaks in the area's education pipeline. It was time for *collective action*—a more closely coordinated *system* of education in and out of school—that would serve every child, every step of the way, from cradle to college and into career.

The Partnership planned a public launch for the summer of 2006. We felt it was important that the start of our collective action commence in a symbolic manner that demonstrated both the boldness of our vision, which was shared and would be carried out by a broad cross-sector group of partners from both sides of the Ohio River, the likes of which the region had never seen.

Among the many bridges that span the Ohio River, only one is purple. Locally referred to as the "Purple People Bridge," its official name is the Newport Southbank Bridge. The bridge has long been closed to vehicle traffic but was repaired and reopened to pedestrian and bicycle traffic only in 2003. Rather than dividing the two states and four neighboring cities, the Purple People Bridge is a strong connector of the vibrant banks on both sides of the river. We felt it would be an ideal spot for our public launch. And so it was. On a sunny August 16, 2006, morning, hundreds of people from both sides of the river met in the middle of the bridge to finally and officially launch the Strive Partnership of Cincinnati and Northern Kentucky.

We knew we needed more than just the roadmap at the launch. Initially they planned to do a landscape analysis of all the resources available to children and youth along the cradle-to-career continuum. But Rob Reifsnyder had seen enough of these in his day that amounted to very little, and he warned the partners not to "asset map our way to nowhere." Based on the very challenging work the United Way had done to launch the Community Impact Agenda that marked a shift for simply funding programs to driving improved outcomes, he recommended we first agree on goals and measures. This would, he noted, give partners a concrete way to measure whether their collective work was actually having an impact.

In hindsight, this decision may have been what enabled the Partnership to stick. The primary focus on outcomes and their sustained improvement was what differentiated this work from previous efforts at collaboration. While those efforts centered on launching new programs or initiatives, this effort would be all about using local data to identify what is really working to improve the overarching outcomes. In all of this work, the central question became: "How do we bring *what works* to scale to move the collective dials that had been stagnant for so long?" The data-driven approach to decision-making CAP embraced has since proved to be the only way to achieve a true collective impact.

In the end, the partners identified five major goals that the Partnership would collectively work to achieve and specific outcomes they would track annually to assess their progress.

Right up until the time of the launch, the Partnership had still been calling itself CAP, a title that marketing experts at Procter & Gamble felt was "too mundane" for the transformative signature effort taking place. In answer, UC's earlier development of the roadmap was expanded to include the larger task of branding, with the UC team ultimately naming and designing all of the materials used at the launch.

"How do we bring what works to scale to move the collective dials that had been stagnant for so long?"

Figure 4.2. Five Major Goals of the Partnership and the Metrics Used to Assess Their Progress

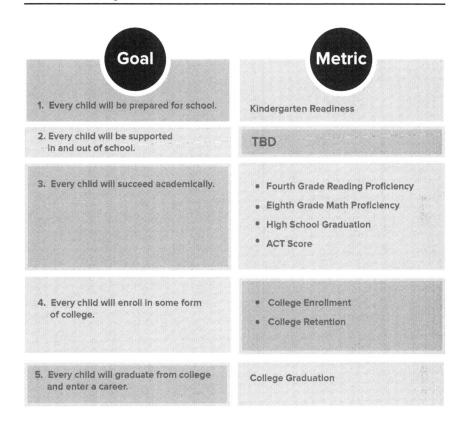

Goal	Metric
1. Every child will be prepared for school.	Kindergarten Readiness
2. Every child will be supported in and out of school.	TBD
3. Every child will succeed academically.	• Fourth Grade Reading Proficiency • Eighth Grade Math Proficiency • High School Graduation • ACT Score
4. Every child will enroll in some form of college.	• College Enrollment • College Retention
5. Every child will graduate from college and enter a career.	College Graduation

Source: Courtesy of Jeff Edmondson and Nancy L. Zimpher

The community was rejuvenated by the launch. In an editorial published that day, the *Cincinnati Enquirer* observed, "This partnership looks like the real deal, and is making us an offer we dare not refuse." A new energy began to ripple through Cincinnati and Northern Kentucky as families, teachers, community leaders, businesses, and others began to view the Strive Partnership with high expectations for the future of their children and the cities in which they lived. The Partnership had been successful in conveying that this was not a program or even a set of programs. It was a system that would facilitate collective, data-driven action for the betterment of the community at large. The Partnership, and the communities it set out to serve, were now primed for that action to start taking place.

BUILDING A CRADLE-TO-CAREER CIVIC INFRASTRUCTURE

Having KWF at the table from the beginning as a "backbone organization" gave the Strive Partnership a critical leg up. This kind of support and infrastructure is critical to any partnership's long-term progress and sustainability. Unlike Cincinnati and Northern Kentucky, most communities that undertake this work do not have this asset in place until a concerted effort to establish one is made.

Pat Brown, a former KWF staff member who then went on to work with Nancy to bring similar initiatives to communities in New York State, spoke of the organization's role in making the effort possible and how its unique mission fosters ideas and innovation from within. "KnowledgeWorks is an operations innovation incubator," she said. "Their mission is to not only provide funding for social innovation but to get involved in the day-to-day operations of the initiatives they funded."

In Cincinnati, KWF's early commitment enabled the Partnership to reach the point of public launch with a backbone staff and fairly sizeable operational budget in place, and it afforded them time to spend focusing on other aspects of the Partnership such as the goals and outcomes. At the time of the launch, the Partnership also had some early in-kind support, with a loaned executive from Procter & Gamble and several point people from UC. There were early funding partners as well in the United Way, Greater Cincinnati Foundation, and Procter & Gamble. In retrospect, the only problem with this backbone support was that it dampened incentive for the Partnership to do any early fundraising, so its broader base of funding partners did not come until much later.

Likewise, it was not until years after the 2006 launch that the Partnership saw the need to define the building blocks, or the core characteristics, that were enabling their work to have an impact where other efforts locally and around the country had previously failed. The group began to refer to it as the process of *building a cradle-to-career civic infrastructure*. In the same way networks of roads and bridges join to create our nation's transportation infrastructure, a new *civic* infrastructure that connected the region's educational schooling and programs with the rest of the services locally that supported the growth of children and families and combined to shape their society's future was the *system* these cross-sector leaders had long been working toward.

Much of the Partnership's success toward having a collective impact was made possible by a collective notion of shared vulnerability and responsibility.

The term "cradle-to-career civic infrastructure" is also meant to define the new kind of leadership we had embraced. Much of the Partnership's success toward having a collective impact was made possible by a collective notion of shared vulnerability and responsibility.

This began to define the collaborative process that had unfolded among them. Still, a more detailed framework was needed to support the momentum we were building, something concrete that could guide the process and keep us on track.

LESSONS LEARNED

Focus on outcomes from the beginning. Organize all work at all levels around these outcomes. They are the true north for all collective work and related decisions.

Don't rush to launch. Let the results speak for themselves to generate a collective sense of progress and purpose.

Find early wins. Use local data to lift up practices that get results for kids.

Share ownership for the work. Make sure the organization providing staff does not chair the partnership. This way it won't be viewed as an organizational initiative.

NOTES

1. Unless otherwise noted, all quotes in the chapter come from interviews with the referenced individuals.

REFERENCES

Cincinnati Public Schools. (2010). Districtwide graduation rate data review. Retrieved from http://www.cps-k12.org/sites/www.cps-k12.org/files/pdfs/aboutGradRate.pdf

Collins, J. (2005). *Good to great and the social sectors: A monograph to accompany Good to Great.* New York, NY: Harper Business.

Greenleaf, R. (2002). *Servant leadership: A journey into the nature of legitimate power and greatness.* 25th anniversary edition. Mahwah, NJ: Paulist Press.

Horn, D. (2001, December 30). 2001: A timeline. *Cincinnati Enquirer.* Retrieved from www.enquirer.com/unrest2001/timeline.html

Korte, G. (2008, July 16). How Cincinnati got segregated. *Cincinnati.com.* Retrieved from news.cincinnati.com/article/20080716/NEWS01/807160314/How-Cincinnati-got-segregated

Ohio History Central. (n.d.). Cincinnati, Ohio. Retrieved from http://www.ohiohistorycentral.org/entry.php?rec=681

Rospert, C. (2012). What is this civic infrastructure? StriveTogether.org blog. Retrieved from http://www.strivetogether.org/blog/2012/08/what-is-this-civic-infrastructure/

Strive Partnership. (2008). *2008 Strive Partnership report card.* Cincinnati: Author.

5

Using Design Thinking to Drive Collective Impact in Higher Education

DAVID J. WEERTS, CHRISTOPHER J. RASMUSSEN, AND VIRAJITA SINGH

ABSTRACT

Colleges and universities are increasingly called upon to be partners in addressing complex social and economic problems in their states and regions. In this context, institutions are moving away from their traditional roles as disciplinary experts and credentialing agents to partners in developing interdisciplinary, cross-sector alliances that tackle persistent societal challenges. In this environment, new ways of thinking are required that capitalize on the knowledge and resources of partnership organizations to drive systemic change. This chapter examines the concept of design thinking for social innovation as a strategy to drive collective impact in higher education.

Colleges and universities are increasingly called upon to play more meaningful roles in contributing to the health and well-being of their regions and society as a whole. In response to these expectations, many institutions are enhancing their public value by working collaboratively across sectors to facilitate social and economic progress in their communities. One prominent example of this collaboration is StriveTogether—a network of public and private-sector organizations working together to support students along their educational pathway. Key goals of the network include boosting kindergarten readiness, raising high school graduation rates, and bolstering college enrollment. Colleges and universities have assumed important roles in this large-scale initiative, which now spans multiple states (Edmondson & Zimpher, 2014). Similarly, the national priority to create a more competitive workforce is spawning new collaborative ventures to boost college completion rates. For example, the National Association of System Heads (NASH) launched an initiative in 2014 called Taking Student Success to Scale (TS3), which aims to produce 350,000 new college graduates by 2025. To date, more than 20 university systems across the country have committed to leveraging their resources toward this effort (National Association of System Heads, 2014). Another example is the newly formed University Innovation Alliance (UIA), which consists of 11 research universities focused on sharing and scaling practices with the goal of making high-quality college degrees accessible to a diverse group of learners. An explicit purpose of the effort is to leverage the strengths and expertise of the UIA to maximize collective impact (University Innovation Alliance, 2014). In announcing the formation of the UIA, Arizona State University president Michael Crow declared, "The next disruption in higher education is collaboration" (Crow, 2014).

Many [colleges and universities] are enhancing their public value by working collaboratively across sectors to facilitate social and economic progress in their communities.

Institutions that are active in these collaborative ventures promote the principles and philosophy of public engagement, which emphasizes a shift away from an expert model of delivering university knowledge to the public toward a more collaborative model in which colleges and their partners co-create knowledge for societal benefit (Boyer, 1996; Kellogg Commission on the Future of State and Land Grant Universities, 1999; New England Resource Center for Higher Education, 2015). Engagement is increasingly viewed as central to the role of higher education in the new century (Fitzgerald, Bruns, Sonka, Furco, & Swanson, 2012) and requires that college and university leaders create imaginative, cooperative postsecondary education institutions that can contribute to these ventures in meaningful ways. Yet it is well known that college cultures and structures are often rigid and unwelcoming to ideas formed outside the walls of academe (Boyte, 2000; Tierney, 2008; Weerts & Sandmann, 2008). As such, institutional leaders and their partners must employ new tools that facilitate relationship building, co-creation, and shared problem solving among diverse entities to bring about significant change. In doing so, knowledge and resources that originate across multiple sectors can be used to drive change processes in a state or region.

The purpose of this chapter is to explore design thinking for social innovation as a strategy for promoting collective impact in a state or region. Our chapter begins with an introduction to design thinking and how it is being used to improve processes and outcomes in various sectors, including higher education. We then more deeply explore design thinking in the higher education context by introducing the Higher Education Redesign Initiative, a Minnesota-based pilot project that engaged scholars, policy makers, students, and corporate and creative industry partners to invent new models to meet changing needs of Minnesota's diverse learners and knowledge-based economy. In this section, we share lessons learned from the project, including ways in which design thinking was employed to develop leadership capacity and promote collective action relative to college access and completion. Finally, we draw on this case example to consider how design thinking might be used as a strategy to drive collective impact in a region or state. In making these contributions, we challenge readers to rethink the role of higher education entities in leading generative thinking that focuses on improving the health and economic vitality of their regions.

WHAT IS DESIGN THINKING?

Design thinking is an emerging field of practice, rooted in the tools and processes traditionally employed in design disciplines (e.g., architecture, landscape architecture, graphic design, interior design, web design, interactive design, etc.). While each of these unique fields takes a nuanced approach to the design process, they share a common methodology. The process of design thinking involves actions such as problem definition, field research, idea generation, storyboarding, frequent prototyping, and narrative as ways to engage participants and motivate creative action.

Design thinking has evolved from the work of many individuals and disciplines, including design, engineering, and the sciences. While the roots of design thinking can be traced back to the 1960s, we focus on the recent history of design thinking and the work of the individuals and organizations that have been most influential in our design initiative. In the 1990s, the work of Silicon Valley design firm IDEO (born from a merger of three industrial design firms) made the notion of design thinking popular in public awareness. The prevalent use of the term *design thinking* is attributed to IDEO founder David M. Kelley. By articulating design terms in easily understood ways and making tools available for open access, Kelley—along with Tim Brown, the current CEO of IDEO—have brought the value of design and design thinking to the public's attention in unprecedented ways (see Brown, 2009; Kelley & Kelley, 2013).

In the 2000s, the notions of design and design thinking were also popularized in the business sectors by Florida (2002), Martin (2009), and Lockwood (2009), among others. In particular, the notion of design as critical to services beyond designed products took root. For example, Pink (2005) proposed that we are moving from an "information age" to a "conceptual age" in which aptitudes of design, story, symphony, empathy, play, and meaning are critical to productivity and success. Around the same time, Stanford University, in collaboration with IDEO, began teaching design thinking as a formal method to its engineering students. This collaborative subsequently became the Hasso Plattner Institute of Design at Stanford (also known as "d.school") and offers immersive programs in design thinking for university students, professionals, and other interested individuals.

Another luminary who can be credited for making design thinking widely known is Toronto-based designer Bruce Mau. In developing his book, *Massive Change*, Mau talked to 100 technicians, thinkers, craftspeople, and laypeople whom he identified as changing the world. Mau saw them as using the word *design* more intelligently and colloquially than designers. With their work's transcendence of traditional professional boundaries, the outcome was a democratization of design, where design was just a critical methodology for solving problems (Mau & Institute without Boundaries, 2004). His provocative, one-page Incomplete Manifesto for Growth (Mau, 2010–2014) also brought design thinking ideas to public attention globally.

In the field of architecture, Tom Fisher, professor and dean of University of Minnesota's College of Design, is considered one of the field's most innovative thinkers and has had a strong influence on the practice of design thinking. His book, *In the Scheme of Things: Alternative Thinking on the Practice of Architecture* (2000), is one of the many writings in which he calls on designers to think beyond their traditional frames and actions. For example, he reminds us, "In a world with little respect for traditional structures, almost

[W]e are moving from an "information age" to a "conceptual age" in which aptitudes of design, story, symphony, empathy, play, and meaning are critical to productivity and success.

everything—from the operation of a company to the organization of a community—can be approached as a design problem" (Fisher, 2000, p. ix).

Evidence abounds that design thinking has been effectively used in a variety of social and organizational contexts to improve processes and outcomes. One prominent example lies in the field of health care. McCreary's (2010) informative piece documents how one design initiative enlisted healthcare providers and patients as collaborators in reducing medical errors. McCreary suggests that design thinking resulted in administrators asking better questions, more clearly defining problems, and ultimately increasing chances of breakthrough solutions. One tangible outcome of the project was the development of a Nurse Knowledge Exchange, which emphasized the exchange of information among nurses and patients at the bedside. The design thinking process revealed that bedside communication was critical to reducing errors and facilitated stronger exchange among patients and healthcare providers.

McCreary (2010) documents how capturing the "untold story" of nurse-patient experiences was critical to finding viable solutions.

Another example of design thinking in a broader social context is illustrated through the work of VisionSpring, a nonprofit organization in India that focuses on affordable access to eyewear. Historically, the organization concentrated its efforts on selling reading glasses to adults, but it sought to expand eye care services and products to children. VisionSpring initiated a design thinking effort focused on understanding the needs of children as they pertain to access to eye care and use of eyewear. The process not only resulted in new eyeglass design but also several services such as children's "eye camps," teacher training relative to children's eye care needs, and transportation for children to receive services. The VisionSpring example is one of many showing how design thinking can lead to real-world solutions that create better outcomes for organizations and the people they serve (Brown & Watt, 2010).

[D]esign thinking resulted in administrators' asking better questions, more clearly defining problems, and ultimately increasing chances of breakthrough solutions.

A NEW WAVE OF DESIGN THINKING IN HIGHER EDUCATION

Design thinking is also making its way into higher education. A recent article in *EDUCAUSE Review* (Morris & Warman, 2015) described several examples of how design thinking has been used to promote student success in college. For instance, at Montgomery Community College, designers sought to address ways in which students could obtain better information about college financial planning. Their efforts resulted in the development of short videos—projected on flat screens around campus—that provided timely, short, and consumable information. In another example, a design team at Ball State University developed an app to promote retention behaviors among Pell grant students. Student participation in the design process led to a new prototype that gamified the app to promote teamwork and competition. Finally, the University of

Maryland University College relied on design thinking to create a pre-enrollment course that facilitated the development of personalized degree plans. Each of these examples illustrates the ways in which design thinking can contribute to student persistence and completion in college (Morris & Warman, 2015).

Other higher education design thinking efforts have gone beyond the individual campus level to facilitate multi-institutional collaborations to promote change in the sector. For example, in 2014, the American Council on Education's Change and Innovation Lab (CIL) employed design thinking to envision new strategies to promote postsecondary education attainment. Funded by the Lumina Foundation, the multicampus initiative focused on developing concrete change strategies related to leadership practices, faculty engagement, and use of data (American Council on Education, 2015). Similarly, the Association of Public and Land-grant Universities (APLU) recently partnered with the Bill and Melinda Gates Foundation and Urban Serving Universities (USU) on the Transformational Planning Grant (TPG) project. TPG is a collaborative of seven institutions that are developing innovative approaches to increase college access, promote student success, and contain costs. Design thinking has been employed by some of the participating institutions to unearth new business models that achieve these goals (Association for Public and Land-grant Universities, 2015; R. Villarreal, personal communication, December 2, 2014).

A MIDWESTERN EXPERIMENT: THE HIGHER EDUCATION REDESIGN INITIATIVE

The preceding examples provide context for a recent Minnesota-based pilot project, the Higher Education Redesign Initiative. The nine-month project engaged scholars, policy makers, students, and corporate/creative industry partners during the 2013–2014 academic year to invent new models to meet the changing needs of Minnesota's diverse learners and knowledge-based economy. In this section we describe the project, lessons learned, and ways in which design thinking has helped to build capacity for collaboration in the region.

The Higher Education Redesign Initiative emerged from discussions about the end of a leadership program that had been administered for several years by the National Center for Public Policy in Higher Education. The National Center's program targeted early-to-mid-career professionals who were engaged in higher education policy in a variety of contexts, including universities, legislatures and other state agencies, foundations, and nonprofit organizations. Cohorts of 12 to 18 "associates" met over three weekends to discuss significant challenges that faced higher education in areas such as access, equity, affordability, and governance. In this process, they built a professional network among each other and with public servants and other policy experts who attended the weekend events.

As participants in the National Center program, two of the authors of this chapter, David Weerts and Chris Rasmussen, envisioned a next-generation model focused on state-level policy that would leverage the assets and imprimatur of their respective organizations: a center at a major public research university focused on higher education innovation (the University of Minnesota's Jandris Center for Innovative Higher Education, jCENTER) and a nonprofit organization deeply engaged with legislators and other public servants across several states (the Midwestern Higher Education Compact, MHEC). The model would build on the National Center program by involving participants in developing solutions to the challenges facing higher education and connecting them with other individuals in their states who possessed the ability to implement these solutions at the state, system, or institution level. In the process of developing this concept, the authors learned about pioneering work underway at the University of Minnesota's Humphrey School of Public Affairs, which had established a unique partnership with the College of Design to employ design thinking to address various challenges facing schools and local communities. Conversations with design thinking expert Virajita Singh and other College of Design leaders resulted in a three-way partnership that connected the College of Design's creative leadership and design expertise with the higher education administration and policy expertise of the jCENTER and MHEC.

Using the National Center cohort model, a pilot program was launched in fall 2013. Eighteen "design associates" were intentionally selected for cross-sector representation from higher education, the nonprofit sector, the private sector, and the creative industries (e.g., architecture, graphic design, and theater and dance) to use design thinking to address perennial challenges facing higher education (e.g., access, affordability, and quality). The mix of participants was intended to reflect the partner entities while recognizing the different approaches employed in various industries and contexts to conceptualize, frame, and solve problems. We also were committed to engaging a wider range of stakeholders—or in design terms, the potential "users" of a product or service—in addressing challenges faced by an industry that very much needs to look outside of itself for any hope of real change.

The program had both process and product objectives. First, we were keen to "test" the format and content of the program—as well as our approach to structuring the cohort—and assess its workability and efficacy for the future. Second, we hoped that the three subgroups—each focused on a specific higher education challenge—would develop prototypes for change that could be (and ideally would be) readily implemented to effect change in higher education. The design associates were given the challenge of how to use open educational resources to (1) address achievement gaps and advance equity in higher education participation and outcomes, (2) reduce cost for students and families, and (3) improve the overall quality of learning.

Our design process drew from the Stanford d.school's concepts of Empathize, Define, Ideate, Prototype, and Test to guide each phase of our design thinking process.[1] Each of the phases was custom designed for each workshop for specific outcomes. Design mindsets or principles are used to inform a design process and to foster the desired dispositions among participants to be successful in the workshops and broader initiative. These mindsets are articulated broadly in the field of design but tailored to each unique challenge and approach. In

The mix of participants was intended to reflect the partner entities while recognizing the different approaches employed in various industries and contexts to conceptualize, frame, and solve problems.

this particular case, we drew on our expertise of our design professional, Virajita Singh, to develop and articulate the appropriate mindsets for this group of designers. Eight mindsets guided group participation relative to the unique design challenge.

Table 5.1. Eight Design Mindsets

1. Embracing diversity in all forms
2. Engaging in radical collaboration
3. Making things visible
4. Demonstrating empathy for the user
5. Expressing creative confidence
6. Having a bias for action
7. Being open to failing forward
8. Committing to iterative action

Over the course of three weekend workshops, the design associates were challenged to practice these eight mindsets while applying principles and practices of design to address their design challenge. The three subgroups worked independently to create an approach to solve some aspect of their designated problem. Prototyping involved multiple iterations of development followed by presentations to other design associates, workshop facilitators, and outside experts. Each presentation was followed by another round of revisions in preparation for yet another set of presentations. At the end of each session, we carefully documented the material that emerged from the process, including recording the voices of participants in describing the evolution of the work. In doing so, we made transparent how ideas from the participants contributed to the direction of outcomes and implementation of the project. The pilot project concluded in June 2014, with design associates' presentation of their prototypes to members of the MHEC governing board, invited guests from foundations and nonprofit organizations, and potential investors. These presentations were delivered with the hope that policy makers and/or entrepreneurs in the audience would consider testing one or more of these prototypes in a regional or statewide context.

PILOT OUTCOMES: THREE PROTOTYPES

The pilot program resulted in several outcomes and lessons that inform our understanding about cross-sector collaboration and creative approaches to problem solving. One key lesson is that design associates across worldviews, fields, sectors, and disciplines challenged each other to look outside the current system to find solutions to the problems at hand. This approach became obvious through the three prototypes that emerged from the pilot. An example of one of the prototypes that emanated from the pilot program is called Ed-visable, a platform that leverages social and professional capital to facilitate college completion and career opportunity for adult students. Drawing on contemporary matchmaking services, Ed-visable combines aspects of an online dating service and a loan shopping program in a way that enables users to match their credentials and skill sets with needs of employers and with postsecondary opportunities. The prototype creates a platform wherein participating colleges and universities can "bid" for the opportunity to evaluate and award academic credit for users' previous college-level work and life experiences (such as military service or other employment). The plan proposes a volunteer network of career and college coaches to facilitate connections in a way that creates a more seamless pathway to degree completion and entry into the workforce. Through its personal network and proposed online platform, the program makes it easier for users to match their interests and skills with opportunities for continuing their education and entering a career.

Another team focused on improving information to prospective students through a holistic community approach to increasing access and public awareness of the higher education opportunities available to individuals. This "Open Ticket" prototype proposed integrating higher education more inextricably into communities by partnering with higher education institutions to create a physical presence directly within neighborhoods alongside other standard services, such as grocery stores, banks, laundromats, and the like. The neighborhood presence is designed to facilitate improved educational opportunities for potential students and their parents/caregivers while promoting the benefits of advanced education to communities. The third team sought to connect individuals with "best fit" education options and to engage immediately in developing networks for career success by matching individuals with mentors to help discover the type of education best suited for their future success. Termed *Grade 99*, the concept focused on providing real-world, hands-on assistance from professionals in the field corresponding with an individual's interests from the start. Meeting learners where they are, and connecting them to resources that have practical application to maximize career outcomes, was a primary focus for this team. The concept would connect higher education institutions and businesses, leveraging resources from each to maximize the individual's access and ability to pursue her or his ideal career, education, and life goals. This team focused on the changing nature of work—both in how individuals change jobs and careers more frequently and how technology changes the way work is completed and approached. Because of the changing nature of work and professional lives, individuals require more professional development and training throughout their careers, and they also need additional education to help facilitate improved access to evolving fields. This team focused on leveraging available resources to facilitate hands-on, experiential learning that increases an individual's ability to change careers and "flow" with the changing tide of the workforce.

The three prototypes struck a chord with policy makers as being responsive to the changing demographics of learners in an increasingly knowledge-based workforce. At least one of the prototypes intrigued one Minnesota state legislator enough that she expressed interest in supporting implementation of the concept. Conversations with this legislator and the design team are ongoing, with the possibility of introducing elements of the prototype into future legislation.

LESSONS LEARNED

While the prototypes themselves yielded intriguing models for future testing, we learned that the success of the pilot was more in the process than in the final products. The design associates praised the opportunity to engage with a cross-section of new colleagues and appreciated the diverse perspectives that they brought to the task. One community college dean described how the design thinking process challenged her to consider problem-solving strategies outside her normal modes of thinking. She explained, "I'm working with people that on a usual basis I probably would not see, and I'm trying to wrap my mind around how different people think and take the strengths from where everybody's coming from and pulling that together." Another design associate and manager at a Minneapolis-based Fortune 500 company expressed her enthusiasm about how resources and knowledge across sectors could be leveraged to make a difference on educational attainment in the region:

> So you have participants from all different sectors coming together to solve one of society's most challenging problems, and that is the problem of accessible, affordable higher education and how we can take this to the next level. . . . The sky's the limit right now, and we as different societal members can solve this together.

A critical outcome of the pilot program has been to develop a network of leaders across sectors who have shared interests around postsecondary education attainment. In the future, this network could be engaged to move this work from design to implementation.

We also note some important challenges and limitations to the design thinking process as it emerged in our pilot project. Each of the prototypes resulted in imaginative models that challenged existing structures and held promise for providing greater value to students and employers. However, design thinking is limited in its ability to address the cultural change that must take place for the prototypes to take root in entrenched contexts. While our design thinking process was careful to incorporate the views of faculty members and other traditional players in the higher education space, the imaginations of a few innovative change agents cannot alone change a deep-rooted system. This challenge became evident within the Grade 99 concept, which called for leveraging existing resources such as technology; open educational resources; and community, industry, and educational partners to

[W]e learned that the success of the pilot was more in the process than in the final products.

seamlessly align students with Minnesota's workforce needs. Part of the proposal called for third-party credentialing, which would give power to an outside entity in certifying skills, knowledge, and competencies of participants related to employer expectations. One university leader in attendance at the final presentations challenged this prototype, declaring that the faculty must have the final word on any modifications to a university-endorsed program that determines credentialing. This comment is illustrative of a traditional view of higher education, which may not consider that emerging public demands and innovations may eventually render a faculty-centric view of higher education obsolete. Disrupting widely held worldviews among stakeholders who are heavily invested in the current system is an ongoing challenge that design thinking may support but not completely address.

As the scale moves to another, broader level, the design of the system must be reconsidered as new users are introduced into the system.

Another challenge that emerged from our design thinking process relates to questions about scale. Since education is no longer a localized function (due to online platforms and other modalities), questions about scope and scale of the initiative were difficult to address. To be implemented successfully, any of the prototypes would require the collaboration of a variety of entities, including institutions and systems, legislatures, businesses, nonprofit organizations, and other community groups. In the end, scale may be mediated by the resources, capacity, and interests of the parties involved. As the scale moves to another, broader level, the design of the system must be reconsidered as new users are introduced into the system. This challenge was identified primarily by policy leaders who were focused on broader impacts of the prototypes.

Despite these challenges, we received feedback that design thinking was valuable in pushing the boundaries of what might be possible in large, rooted systems such as higher education. Upon conclusion of the pilot, many of the design associates told us how they had used the concepts in their own work. Two design associates even reconfigured a planned annual workshop for nonprofit professionals to employ a design thinking approach. Similar feedback was received from presentations made at a conference of state higher education agency representatives, who saw our work as an example of how to improve the success of efforts in planning and change within institutions and systems. While more experimentation and testing are necessary, the pilot project yielded important outcomes worth pursuing in other higher education contexts.

CAN DESIGN THINKING FACILITATE COLLECTIVE IMPACT?

Thus far, our chapter has described the concept of design thinking and how it might be a tool to address innovation and change in higher education. In this final section, we translate how design thinking methods may relate to collective impact efforts in a community, state, and regional context. In the end, we give particular emphasis to how higher education entities might lead these processes.

Kania and Kramer (2011) define collective impact as long-term commitments by a range of stakeholders across sectors around a common agenda focused on social change. They suggest that collective impact is a compelling approach that may help to overcome the failings of existing strategies aimed to produce broad social change. Specifically, Kania and Kramer lament that various social institutions continue to be focused on individual, often isolated, interventions that have limited impact. After describing successful efforts that have yielded positive results, they conclude that "large-scale social change comes from better cross-sector coordination rather than from the isolated intervention of individual organizations" (p. 12).

Kania and Kramer (2011) suggest that the key elements of collective impact strategy consist of a centralized infrastructure, a dedicated staff, and a structured process that leads to a common agenda, shared measurement, continuous communication, and mutually reinforcing activities among all participants. In particular, collective impact requires a shared vision for change. This process may require candid discussions about differences that must be resolved to move toward a shared goal. Finally, the authors emphasize the importance of having a backbone organization that can manage and facilitate the process. This component is central to the sustainability and success of the collective impact strategy.

Based on the results of our pilot project, we suggest that these collective impact strategies could benefit greatly from design thinking practices. As discussed earlier in this chapter, the Higher Education Redesign Initiative was predicated on the idea of engaging diverse entities to address a common problem. Similar to what Kania and Kramer (2011) articulate, our process required negotiation and candid discussions among design associates about how to reach viable and actionable solutions. For example, program participants held a range of views about how to finance and sustain the prototypes upon implementation. Some passionately argued that users of the services were likely to be poor and underserved and suggested that the proposed programs should be funded exclusively by government or foundation sources. Meanwhile, others proposed business models that required users to pay a fee in accessing services. Groups hashed out business plans that sought to strike a balance in how participants viewed the financing question. The eight design mindsets identified earlier in this chapter became the basis on which the three teams moved forward on building consensus and achieving a common goal.

Our process revealed that design thinking processes can build the leadership capacity necessary to sustain a collective impact initiative. We found that the Higher Education Redesign Initiative resulted in a new community of practice in which participants developed common approaches to problem solving. As such, the Twin Cities region has expanded its group of community leaders who have the skills to work together on complex social problems. We noted that the Higher Education Redesign Initiative helped to build cohesion and camaraderie among a group of individuals with different worldviews and problem-solving strategies. This bonding process was not immediate, as group work was contentious at times, especially in the early stages. This was especially evident as some participants came in with strongly held political ideologies that guided their thinking. By practicing the eight design mindsets, groups worked through this tension and arrived at cohesion. It is known that collective impact initiatives require cohesion among group leaders and participants, and the design thinking process can play a role in creating an innovative community that can focus on shared goals.

Importantly, design thinking processes result in products or prototypes for action. The Higher Education Redesign Initiative process netted actionable solutions based on a concrete set of design challenges. Similarly, collective impact strategies are focused on making measurable changes in communities by changing systems, practices, and policies. Design thinking emphasizes the user experience and thus focuses on empathic interviews with those most impacted by the system. As was noted earlier in this chapter, healthcare professionals who employ design thinking engage the perspectives of patients and nurses to change the system. In the Higher Education Redesign Initiative, we sought the views of students and families who have firsthand experiences of barriers to degree completion and attainment. We suggest that collective impact strategies will be most effective when they are guided by a deep knowledge of the communities that they are trying to support. Through empathic interviews and other strategies, design thinking provides an avenue for collective impact leaders to remain grounded in the needs of their community.

[C]ollective impact initiatives require cohesion among group leaders and participants, and the design thinking process can play a role in creating an innovative community that can focus on shared goals.

In closing, we make the case that higher education entities—individual campuses, systems, and regional compacts—can play an important leadership role in facilitating these design processes for collective impact. Our experience with the Higher Education Redesign Initiative revealed the strength of partnership in joining leaders across two university colleges and a regional higher education compact to lead this process. Along the way, we realized that our three-way collaboration was in itself an innovative experiment that required building trust and understanding one another's worlds. Yet given the unique roles of MHEC, jCENTER, and the College of Design in the higher education and social innovation space, we created and nurtured a partnership that focused on our shared interests in the region. We suggest that other structures, such as statewide higher education systems, may see themselves in similar roles as facilitators and conveners to support collective impact ventures via design thinking. Our experience suggests that design mindsets and practices offer a fruitful approach to building leadership capacity and creating innovative new models that support state and regional goals.

ACKNOWLEDGMENTS

We are grateful to Larry Isaak, president of Midwestern Higher Education Compact; Jean Quam, dean of University of Minnesota College of Education and Human Development; and Tom Fisher, dean of University of Minnesota College of Design, all of whom generously supported the Higher Education Redesign Initiative pilot program.

NOTE

1. See Hasso Plattner Institute of Design at Stanford University, *An Introduction to Design Thinking Process Guide*, available at dschool.stanford.edu.

REFERENCES

American Council on Education. (2015). *Change and innovation lab*. Retrieved from http://www.acenet.edu/news-room/Pages/Change-and-Innovation-Lab-Main-Page.aspx

Association of Public and Land-grant Universities. (2014). *Transformational planning grant*. Retrieved from http://www.aplu.org/TPG

Boyer, E. L. (1996). The scholarship of engagement. *Journal of Higher Education Outreach and Engagement 1*(1), 11–20.

Boyte, H. C. (2000). *Public engagement in a civic mission: A case study*. Washington, DC: Council on Public Policy Education.

Brown, T. (2009). *Change by design: How design thinking transforms organizations and inspires innovation.* New York, NY: HarperCollins.

Brown, T., & Watt, J. (2010, Winter). Design thinking for social innovation. *Stanford Social Innovation Review.* Retrieved from http://www.ssireview.org/articles/entry/design_thinking_for_social_innovation

Crow, M. (2014). *The next disruption in higher education is collaboration.* Retrieved from Arizona State University website: http://president.asu.edu/node/1449

Edmondson, J., & Zimpher, N. L., (2014). *Striving together: Early lessons in achieving collective impact in education.* Albany, NY: State University of New York Press.

Fisher, T. (2000). Design in a world of flows. In *In the scheme of things: Alternative thinking on the practice of architecture* (pp. 1–12). Minneapolis, MN: University of Minnesota Press.

Fitzgerald, H. E., Bruns, K., Sonka, S. T., Furco, A., & Swanson, L. (2012). The centrality of engagement in higher education. *Journal of Higher Education Outreach and Engagement* 16(1), 149–167.

Florida, R. (2002). *The rise of the creative class: And how it's transforming work, leisure and everyday life.* New York, NY: Basic Books.

Kania, J., & Kramer, M. (2011, Winter). Collective impact. *Stanford Social Innovation Review.* Retrieved from http://www.ssireview.org/articles/entry/collective_impact

Kelley, T., & Kelley, D. (2013). *Creative confidence: Unleashing the creative potential within us all.* New York, NY: Crown Business.

Kellogg Commission on the Future of State and Land Grant Universities. (1999). *Returning to our roots: The engaged institution.* Retrieved from Association of Public and Land-grant Universities website: http://www.aplu.org/NetCommunity/Document.Doc?id=183

Lockwood, T. (Ed.). (2009). *Design thinking: Integrating innovation, customer experience and brand value.* New York, NY: Allworth Press.

Martin, R. L. (2009). *The design of business: Why design thinking is the next competitive advantage.* Boston, MA: Harvard Business Press.

Mau, B. (2010–2014). An incomplete manifesto for growth. Retrieved from Manifesto Project: http://www.manifestoproject. it/bruce-mau/

Mau, B., & Institute without Boundaries. (2004). *Massive change.* London: Phaidon Press.

McCreary, L. (2010, September). Kaiser Permanente's innovation on the front lines. *Harvard Business Review*, 1–6.

Morris, H. E., & Warman, G. (2015). Using design thinking in higher education. *EDUCAUSE Review*. Retrieved from http://www. educause.edu/ero/article/using-design-thinking-higher-education

National Association of System Heads (December 4, 2014). National Association of System Heads calls for at least 350,000 more college graduates in 10 years. Retrieved from http://www. nashonline.org/news

New England Resource Center for Higher Education (NERCHE). (2015). Carnegie community engagement classifications. Retrieved from http://nerche.org/index.php?option=com_content &view=article&id=341&Itemid=92

Pink, D. H. (2005). *A whole new mind: Why right-brainers will rule the future.* New York, NY: Riverhead.

Tierney, W. G. (2008). *The impact of culture on organizational decision-making: Theory and practice in higher education.* terling, VA: Stylus.

University Innovation Alliance. (2014). Our work. Retrieved from http://www.theuia.org/#our-work

Weerts, D. J., & Sandmann, L. R. (2008). Building a two-way street: Challenges and opportunities for community engagement at research universities. *Review of Higher Education 32*(1), 73–106.

6

THE ALBANY PROMISE STORY

*How a Community Came Together to
Go All-in on Education Reform*

JULIETTE PRICE

ABSTRACT

Albany Promise is a cradle-to-career partnership that is working
to change the educational outcomes of youth in a high-poverty,
urban setting through collective impact. This chapter describes how
the community came together to create a shared vision for success
and how the local higher education sector supported the initiative.

Education reform is famous for being either ruthlessly driven
from the top down or driven upward via grassroots work. Both
models have shown varying degrees of success, with wide-scale educational reform eluding many who attempt it. Most initiatives are
also either siloed within education or attempt to bring in one other
sector—perhaps government or industry—to try to fix the problems
that education faces. Rarely has an entire community—leaders in
early childhood, K–12, and postsecondary education; business and
industry; government; faith-based groups, and nonprofit organizations—come together to wrap its arms around the complicated
issues that face urban education in the 21st century. Even fewer

communities have given up the old way of doing business—what "feels right" or "what we've always done"—in favor of rigorously using data to drive decision making for students. And perhaps even fewer communities have committed to using continuous quality-improvement tools to measure progress every step of the way and hold themselves accountable to changing the outcomes for the success of every child.

This is the story of Albany Promise, the cradle-to-career educational partnership that is tackling these very issues in the heart of the City of Albany, New York. It is a story of leadership, data, and collaborative efforts to finally reverse the disheartening cycle of low educational attainment and poverty in a city like so many others in our country, where the American Dream seems to slip further and further out of reach for so many. It is also a story of how higher education has bravely stepped out of its ivory tower to take on work not traditionally seen as its own, and how a community learned to work together. It is ultimately a story of how one community has chosen to go all-in, prioritizing the future of its children above all individual agendas.

> **[Few] communities have given up the old way of doing business—what "feels right" or "what we've always done"—in favor of rigorously using data to drive decision making for students.**

THE ALBANY STORY

The Europeans first discovered the area in the early 1600s when Henry Hudson came upon it when searching for faster trade routes in the New World. First established by the Dutch, the Albany region remains one of the oldest surviving settlements of the original 13 colonies. During the late 18th century, Albany was one of the 10 most populated cities in the United States, becoming a major hub of transportation due to its valuable location on the Hudson River. The city also boasted some of the earliest railroad systems in the country, allowing goods and services to make their way from the Erie Canal to the Hudson River to the railroad and onward to the rest of the United States. As transportation innovations accelerated, however, Albany began to fall behind, and by the close of the 19th century, its population had dropped, and other cities in New York began to outpace the population of the state capital.

In the second half of the 20th century, Albany experienced the tenure of the longest-serving mayor of any city in the United States, Erastus Corning. For 41 years, Corning ruled the city, but even admirers struggle to name major accomplishments of his lengthy term. His preference for the status quo did not help the city to navigate changing urban dynamics in the mid-1900s. During the 1950s and 1960s, Albany lost more than 20% of its population as suburbs sprawled away from the city, and business and industry moved out. Unlike other cities facing similar issues, Albany's leadership seemed unconcerned about the imminent problems it was facing. A strong and notoriously corrupt Democratic political machine, housed in the state's capital, also did not help, giving Albany its oft-cited title "the capital of corruption" (Grondahl, 2007). Meanwhile, Governor Nelson Rockefeller, who served from 1959 to 1973, had a taste for the grandiose and ordered large, government-sponsored building projects, including the creation of the Empire State Plaza, which destroyed entire city blocks and evicted over 9,000 residents from their homes under the auspices of eminent domain. Entire parks, schools, small businesses, and neighborhoods were lost, splitting Albany geographically and disconnecting poor and minority populations.

At the close of the 20th century, Albany found itself a tattered version of what it once was. Financially strained due to the large amount of government and nontaxable land, a shrinking number of city residents, and the departure of businesses and industries from the high-tax state, the city faced severe issues. As the seat of state government, nearly two-thirds of the daily workforce was a population that drove in from the suburbs and exited at the end of the workday. The resident population did not necessarily benefit from the churning of state work and was often overlooked in state-sponsored projects or initiatives. Larger cities in New York State that also face dire circumstances, such as Buffalo, Rochester, or Yonkers, tend to attract more attention because of their larger populations and consequent higher number of elected officials.

As a result of these circumstances, a heavy concentration of Albany's residents live in poverty, without many ladders in place for them to climb their way into a better life. Education, and its empowering effects, remains one of the best tools to end cyclical poverty, yet the educational attainment of residents remains disturbingly low. Many of the schools in the City School District of Albany are labeled as "failing" according to the State Education Department; some schools have been on this list for over 10 years. The poor outcomes for students are compounded by the complications of poverty; the established system of education works well for middle-class, nonminority students, not for the majority of minority, low-income students who most urgently need the system to work for them. For these children, classroom size and the level of rigor of instruction are not the only bumps on the road to success. The bumps include greater issues of urban survival—inadequate housing, food insecurity, and all the challenges of perduring poverty. In short, the system is designed to get exactly what it is getting, and the children of Albany are left at a severe disadvantage.

With such a dire outlook for such a large percentage of the city's population, there was nowhere to go but up. Through a committed group of leaders, and a lot of elbow grease, the stage was set to begin tackling this immense education problem.

Today, Albany is home to just under 100,000 New Yorkers, 25% of whom are 19 years old or younger. The city's population remains majority white (56%), with a large minority group identifying as black (33%). An additional 6% of residents identify as Asian, and 9% of the population identifies as Hispanic/Latino (independent of race). The demography of the City School District of Albany is quite different from the citywide population. Enrollment in the district nears 10,000 students, with 68% identifying as either black or Hispanic, 23% as white, and 9% as Asian. As in most urban settings, economic indicators are uneven across the city, with poverty estimates ranging from 7% in some zip codes to 58% in others. Per capita income ranges from approximately

Figure 6.1. Economic Indicators of Students in the City School District of Albany

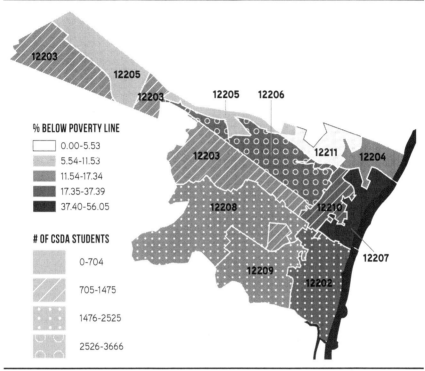

Source: American Community Survey 5-year Estimates (2009–2013)

$11,000 to $35,000 across neighborhoods in Albany. The poverty rate for all city residents stands at 25%. This figure rises above 30% among children and reaches 36% for children under five. Poverty climbs even higher in single-parent households, rising above 40%. Children, ages 17 and younger, are disproportionally concentrated in the poorest areas of the city (The Albany Promise, 2014).

The unemployment rate in Albany is 10%, representing about 5,000 individuals. City residents 25 years old and older have varying levels of educational attainment, with 38% having a high school diploma or lower; 17% having some college but no degree; 8%

having an associate's degree; and 37% having a bachelor's degree or higher (The Albany Promise, 2014).

With such a dire outlook for such a large percentage of the city's population, there was nowhere to go but up. Through a committed group of leaders, and a lot of elbow grease, the stage was set to begin tackling this immense education problem.

THE LEADERSHIP EQUATION

As the new millennium opened in Albany, so did several key windows of opportunity. In 2010, New York State's 56th race for the governorship brought a serious candidate into the spotlight and eventually into office. Andrew M. Cuomo, son to New York's 52nd governor, came into power after a series of embarrassing gubernatorial scandals, bringing with him a mantra of "performance, integrity, and pride."

Just one short year earlier, the State University of New York (SUNY) system, with 64 campuses and over 465,000 students across the state, had conducted a year-long search for a new chancellor to lead the system. The Board of Trustees saw the chance to reinvigorate the system through a leader who could harness the power of such a large network of incredibly diverse colleges and universities. Enter Nancy L. Zimpher, the Board's choice to take over the sprawling system. Zimpher, who previously served as president of the University of Cincinnati, had a history of placing huge importance on partnership and collective impact. She had acted as the original convener of the Cincinnati Strive Partnership, which connected the K–12 system to higher education and the community, changing educational outcomes across an entire city (see chapter 4). Zimpher hit the ground running, and in the summer of 2009, she visited each of the system's 64 campuses and pulled together a core group of stakeholders, affectionately called the Group of 200, to build SUNY's strategic plan for the future. Surfacing from the Great Recession of 2008, the plan called for both economic revitalization and improving the quality of life for every New Yorker. The plan was broken into six Big Ideas, and unsurprisingly, one focused on connecting the dots to improve education across the entire cradle-to-career pipeline.

The City School District of Albany was also facing a changing of the guard. Like so many urban school districts, superintendent turnover was fairly rapid, with most serving between three and five years. After a tumultuous few years in the early 2000s during which Albany became ground zero for charter schools (mostly due to its proximity to the state's capital, where policy and funding are decided), the city's board of education launched a national search for a new leader to help the district turn around its 12 failing schools. In 2012, the district welcomed Marguerite Vanden Wyngaard, formerly the deputy superintendent in Paterson, New Jersey.

Two more key leadership positions were also poised for renewal. First, the president of the State University of New York at Albany announced his retirement in 2011, opening a national search for a new leader A year later, in 2012, the university announced that Robert J. Jones would take the helm. Jones had spent the last 34 years at the University of Minnesota, serving as senior vice president for academic administration for the system, arming him with a deep knowledge of system reform and how to drive powerful results at scale. In Minnesota, he was widely known for his deep commitment to community engagement, notably around improving educational outcomes for poor and minority students. He had convened a table of key stakeholders in Minnesota, called Generation Next, to work together around these issues.

The mayor's office had hosted the same occupant for 20 years in 2013—the perpetual joke about Albany's forever mayor moving closer and closer to reality. But in 2013, the city's treasurer and outspoken advocate for the disenfranchised put in a bid for the office. The sitting mayor announced that he was not running for reelection, and Kathy Sheehan overwhelmingly won the primary and general election for mayor. In January 2014, Albany welcomed its first female mayor.

Change was in the air, and the excitement surrounding new leadership was palpable, bringing new energy and optimism to the community. While leadership is not singularly important to collective impact initiatives, it is a large driving force at the beginning of any large-scale change effort. The changing of the guard can provide the sense that it is a "good time" to begin to work differently, as old habits move on with their old leaders. Later in the chapter, it will be outlined how leadership transition during a collective impact initiative that is in full-swing can be problematic, and tactics are discussed that can be used to ensure that new leaders do not derail existing work.

A COMMUNITY RALLIES TOGETHER

In 2010 and 2011, the U.S. Department of Education released applications for Promise Neighborhood grants—a new framework for education reform through which successful applicants would attempt a place-based strategy of choosing very small areas of a city on which to focus and improve educational outcomes by working deeply with the residents of the area (U.S. Department of Education, 2015). A small group of committed citizens, frustrated by the lack of improvement in the school district and the perceived lack of leadership in the city, banded together and began to meet to see if Albany could win a grant. In 2010, the application was rejected. In 2011, the group asked SUNY to be the lead applicant, hoping that the influence of a large university could help their bid. The 2011 application came back negative again.

Zimpher had at this point become familiar with Albany and its leaders, hopes, and dreams. The idea of educational renewal in a city where less than half of its graduating class crossed the stage in June appealed to a number of the leaders with whom she met. Her well-known track record and her personality inspired many to ask her what could be done in the state's capital city. The air was charged with potential, with so many new and energetic leaders who were committed to turning Albany's potential energy into kinetic energy. Zimpher gathered key partners who had worked on the prior grant applications and presented them with the Strive framework, which was not so different from what the group aimed to do if it received a Promise Neighborhood grant. The catch was the leaders would have to do the work with

It was not the lack of dollars that was failing the system. Rather, it was the lack of process, data, and collective impact.

the money that was already being invested in education and what little more the partners could scrape together. But Zimpher was clear: It was not the lack of dollars that was failing the system. Rather, it was the lack of process, data, and collective impact. The group responded positively, and it was clear that allegiance was not toward any specific model but toward delivering different results for the children of the City of Albany.

Slowly, the small group began to grow as more partners were invited to the table and more organizations began hearing about the group's vision. The meetings expanded until they occurred in a local church's assembly room, with rows and rows of tables and cups and cups of coffee. Monthly meetings, held at 7:30 in the morning, would attract a hundred participants eager to get to work. The biggest priorities become figuring out 1) what the partnership would look like; 2) what were the biggest areas of concern; and 3) how the new collective would go about addressing them.

SETTING A VISION

As the massive meetings continued to attract more partners, it became clear that each individual was bringing a personal agenda to the table. Some participants thought that the answer to the city's education woes lay in boosting the quality of early child care. Others believed that it was in strengthening the high school curriculum. The rigor of tutoring offered. The lack of uniforms. After-school programming. Parental involvement. Prenatal vitamins. The list was long and getting longer by the minute, with each partner sure that he or she had *the* answer. Not unlike other partnerships across the nation, the group simply did not know where to begin. Someone affectionately mentioned that it felt as though each partner was so busy mopping the floor that no one was busy turning off the faucet, meaning that the lack of coordination or high-flying vision were contributing to the mess.

In one meeting, to better illustrate what the partnership was trying to do, a large roll of butcher paper was tacked onto a wall. On it was the cradle-to-career timeline, starting at birth and ending at career. Partners were given Post-it notes and were instructed to write down programs that they provided to students and families. They then stuck their notes on the timeline at the proper age point. Twenty minutes later, the paper was completely covered in bright squares. The group stepped back and was silent for a few moments, until one partner exclaimed, "We're doing all that, and nothing's working for our kids! How is this possible?"

As the group discussed and prioritized and reprioritized, the partnership staff began to push the group to think about impact. For example, we knew that there were early childhood education providers in the community, but did we know what the impact was on children who attend their programs? How effective were the tutoring options offered to students? Did we understand how the high school curriculum affected college readiness rates? The group members realized quickly that they were completely in the dark when it came to impact. Almost no data were available, and when they were, they typically were high-level, annual data that could not be used to make smaller, incremental changes.

The first big lift that the partnership staff undertook was to gather all available data and condense it into one readable report. Before the partnership could decide on priority areas, it needed to better understand the entire education landscape. The report was wide-ranging and included data from pre-K to college enrollment rates. Once the report was compiled, the partners took a look—and heaved a collective sigh. No section of the report was particularly encouraging, and student achievement was fairly stagnant at each part of the pipeline. Quickly, the partners chose 20 outcome areas—points along the cradle-to-career continuum where they wanted to focus their work, where they felt that if they could get those things right, the children of Albany would achieve different outcomes. From there, the partnership narrowed its focus to just a few outcome areas: kindergarten readiness; third and fourth

The group members realized quickly that they were completely in the dark when it came to impact. Almost no data were available, and when they were, they typically were high-level, annual data that could not be used to make smaller, incremental changes.

Figure 6.2. Current Action Team Areas

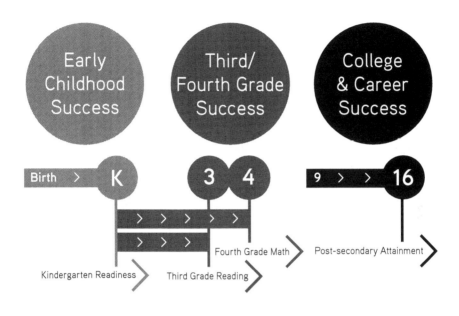

Source: 2014 Albany Promise Report Card

grade success; and high school, college, and career readiness. This basic framework set the stage for the partnership to start its work. It had a roadmap for the path that it wanted for all students to take and, from there, priority outcome areas for them to achieve. It was time to launch.

DIGGING IN

With the baseline report to the community in hand, the partnership decided it was time to bring the initiative to the public. Two launch events were planned for May 7, 2012. The first would take place during the day, for the press and the partnership leaders, and the second would happen during the evening, in an attempt to engage residents and families. With all the major partners onstage, the partnership was launched with much fanfare—the community members in attendance seemed cautiously optimistic that this kind of partnership could help to solve the pervasive issues that had plagued Albany for so long.

With newly acquired public attention in hand, the partnership staff began to convene action teams—small working groups that would begin to concentrate on a specific outcome area and identify potential solutions to the issues at hand. Each action team was composed of providers, experts, and policy makers who worked in the area of focus. For example, the early childhood action team was made up of infant, toddler, and pre-K providers (e.g., center directors, teachers, district coordinators); experts in early childhood pedagogy; county-level child and family services staff members; family support providers; teacher preparation experts from higher education institutions; pediatric healthcare providers; and parent representatives. This cross-sector group was able to address problems and difficult issues that none of their individual institutions could solve alone.

Action teams met frequently, every two weeks for two hours at a time, which was intended to ensure that the results stay in the forefront of each partner's daily priorities and that movement toward improving the chosen indicator could happen in six months or a year. Partners were often initially surprised at how much of a commitment the action teams were—in typical collaborations, partners may only meet every few months and usually spend the bulk of their time together updating each other on what they individually are doing. This program required a major shift to move partners to an understanding of how collective impact is different from collaboration: Change in everyday practice is what moves the dial, and to get there, time is the currency of investment.

Just like teams in the workplace or on an athletic field, action teams took time to form, storm, norm, and perform, following Tuckman's (1965) model. Often, the newly formed teams were composed of colleagues who may not have ever met or worked together. This lack of familiarity did not mean that team members did not already have preconceived notions of each other's institutions or work—in fact, this was regularly the case. Membership on a team that includes folks whom one may have regularly blamed for being "part of the problem" forces partners to stop pointing fingers at or placing blame on others. New teams often spent a few initial months building trust between members, typically in the form of asset mapping and data sharing, an informal way of sharing each other's vulnerabilities and shortcomings. More often than not, poor communication, or a complete lack of communication, between the partners had built false narratives of who did what or who had not been a good steward of students and families. Through the shared vulnerability that was established at the action team level, partners entered a new phase of partnership and trust, which enabled them to break through years (sometimes decades) of hurt feelings and begin working together.

Change in everyday practice is what moves the dial, and to get there, time is the currency of investment.

A critical part of building trust came through the process of establishing a charter for each action team. Charters drew very strict lines in the sand with regard to what the action team would work on, as well as what the team would not address. They included defining the problem and its scope, targets, and operating principles.

This clear delineation of boundaries, authority, roles, and tasks allowed group members to hold each other accountable without having to revisit these concepts each time they met. For a group of people who did not report to anyone at the partnership directly and did not have any traditional power over each other, this arrangement was extremely important. At any moment, the thread that held these stakeholders together could snap, and the clarity of all of these pieces was key for keeping each of the key players at the table.

PROCESS IS THE NEW PROGRAM

Since the partnership was not a direct service provider, and each of the providers sat at the action team level, the immediate question that arose became: What does this partnership do differently

THE ALBANY PROMISE

EARLY CHILDHOOD ACTION TEAM CHARTER

Purpose Statement

This team is comprised of over 25 members representing agencies, service providers, and educational institutions dedicated to increasing the percentage of students in the targeted neighborhoods who have the skills needed for success in kindergarten, as measured by kindergarten intake assessment.

Problem Statement

While 88% of children in the target neighborhoods[1] are enrolled in a variety of early learning settings,[2] many are entering kindergarten lacking basic reading readiness skills. Early childhood settings are critical to building the foundations for learning, which all students need to begin a successful journey through the K–12 system.

National research suggests that the achievement gap is visible even at the kindergarten level, with students from disadvantaged backgrounds showing gaps in early reading and mathematics skills, oral language development, vocabulary, and general knowledge.[3] Studies show the difficulty of catching students up in the higher grades, leaving them unable to meet college and career readiness benchmarks in high school.[4] Simply put, the work of ensuring an equitable educational foundation for all students begins in early childhood.

Data on the various early learning settings in Albany are limited and oftentimes are incompatible with other sources. More specifically, it is not clear which curriculum, practices, guidelines, and assessments are being used across the settings, if any. Further exacerbating the problem are the disparities of professional credentials and training within various early learning settings. Community efforts to engage families as the providers of the first learning environment are limited and disconnected. Additionally, not all children are screened at regular intervals to ensure that their social, emotional, and nutritional development is on track, which is critical to early learning success in schools.

Project Scope

The focus of this team is to identify effective strategies that raise kindergarten readiness across all early childhood learning settings, in the community, and with families. As detailed in the team's kindergarten success definition, it is the collective responsibility of all three of these groups to ensure all students are kindergarten ready to learn.

The team understands that there are a variety of variables that negatively impact kindergarten readiness, such as level of parents' education, which are out of the action team's scope of control. Data on these variables will be tracked as contextual indicators and referred to other networks when appropriate.

Targets

Long-term target: By 2017, increase the percentage of children meeting kindergarten readiness benchmarks by 35% (baseline 2014 data + 35%).

Operating Principles

The Early Childhood Success Action Team is aligned with the goals of the Albany Promise Cradle-to-Career Partnership and agrees to:

- Ensure action team goals and activities focus on the needs of the early childhood community.
- Respect and listen to action team members, and think beyond the capacity of individual organizations and services.
- Collaborate by sharing and using data, information, and research to drive decision making and achieve action team goals.
- Communicate in a way that promotes accurate and timely dissemination of information to action team members, enables evidence-based decision making, and maintains appropriate confidentiality.
- Attend and participate in all meetings, carry out assigned tasks, and support implementation of action plan.

Notes

1. The Albany Promise target neighborhoods are Arbor Hill, South End, and West Hill.
2. Universal Pre–K, Head Start, child care.
3. Betty Hart and Todd R. Risley, *Meaningful Differences in the Everyday Experience of Youth American Children* (Baltimore, MD: Paul H. Brookes, 1995).
4. ACT, *Forgotten Middle: Ensuring That All Students Are on Target for College and Career Readiness before High School*, https://www.act.org/research/policymakers/pdf/ForgottenMiddle.pdf

or additionally from what each individual provider is doing? The secret sauce of the partnership lies in process and process improvement. To illustrate this point, I present the early childhood action team as an example.

When originally convened, the early childhood action team had to define the scope of its work. Early childhood refers to the first five years of a child's life, until the moment the child enters kindergarten. Research has furthered our understanding of early brain development, with some studies showing that a significant amount of brain development happens during these first formative years (Shonkoff & Phillips, 2000). With this knowledge in hand, one would think that early childhood education would be rigorously designed and managed. Sadly, the truth is far from this assumption. Within the City of Albany, there existed over 100 early childhood education providers—some large and well funded; some smaller and serving only a handful of students; and others operating what are known as legally exempt, or informal, childcare centers, where fewer than eight children are being cared for by a provider. This small type of operation is exempt from state certification requirements. The variance in quality is overwhelming and can negatively impact the readiness of five-year-olds for kindergarten. Many of the children with weaker early child care experiences arrive at school with a smaller range of skills, which impacts their ability to make adequate progress on the path to the key academic skills they will need during the key early years of elementary school.

The team members quickly decided that tackling the entire birth through year 5 continuum was too much, so they prioritized working on the year before kindergarten, pre-K. Immediately the lack of data became apparent—unfortunately, New York State does not have a definition of kindergarten readiness or require a kindergarten readiness assessment. This policy means that kindergarten teachers, based on their expertise and knowledge base, are probably the only ones who can identify which students are ready for kindergarten work and which are not—not a particularly effective way to begin working toward improvement. The team collaborated to establish a local kindergarten readiness definition, which included specific roles for early childhood providers, families, and the broader community.

KINDERGARTEN SUCCESS FORMULA

Albany Promise and its members are committed to working together to ensure the success of all incoming kindergarteners, with the knowledge that: all children are capable of learning; all children develop at different rates; and success necessitates collaboration between families, communities, and schools to ensure the success of every child.

Kindergarten Success Formula
Families + Community + Programs = Children Ready for Success in Kindergarten

Families: Families provide loving, stable, and healthy environments for children; engage in positive play and learning experiences with children; recognize their role as the child's first teacher and advocate.

Programs: Programs engage the child where they are developmentally; meet high-quality care, educational, and developmental benchmarks; meet the diverse learning needs of all children; focus on both social-emotional and academic development; focus on progress in a child's learning; and partner with families to help each child reach her or his potential.

Community: The community provides access to high-quality early learning opportunities; provides accessible health care for all children; and provides a vast array of learning experiences in the community for children that builds critical learning skills.

Next, the team identified the lack of data as a high-priority project. The registration process for incoming kindergarten students lacked questions about whether the children had attended pre-K or any form of preschool—an easy fix that the team quickly remedied to have a better idea of how many students were coming into kindergarten with any formal school exposure. Next, the team attacked the lack of assessment data. From third grade reading rates and anecdotal evidence provided by instructional leaders, the team knew that certain students were entering without the skills necessary to make them proficient readers by third grade. After all, if some students were coming in two or three years behind, even exceptional teachers would struggle to bring a child to proficiency. With the expertise of an English language arts specialist in the district, the team quickly designed and administered the district's first-ever kindergarten readiness assessment, measuring each student's readiness in six key literacy areas. To no surprise, the results were not stellar, but they provided a much clearer roadmap of the skills that needed to be addressed in pre-K.

Another area of focus that the team quickly identified was the need to support pre-K providers with high-quality professional development for their teaching staffs. Unless they were large and well-funded, programs did not have the resources to pay for professional development of their staff members. Immediately, a partner at the table, the regional provider of such high-quality early childhood training, stepped up and offered monthly trainings at no cost

Figure 6.3. City School District of Albany 2014 Kindergarten Assessment Results

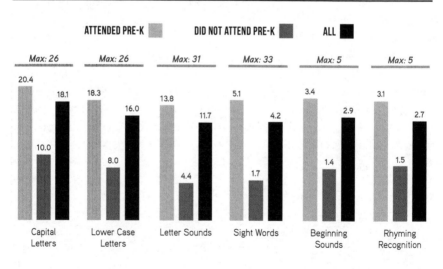

Source: 2014 Albany Promise Report Card

to providers, even offering the attendees the professional development credits that they need to remain in good standing with the state's certification process. The strategy worked, and within six months, the trainings had served 55 teachers from 22 programs across Albany. In the next year, the team expanded, offering monthly professional development trainings to infant, toddler, and pre-K providers. In nine months, over 97 teachers were served, and program directors reported changed practices within their programs.

Through the relationship building that was happening at each of these sessions, a common theme began to emerge. Many programs lacked a research-based curriculum and assessment system, meaning that at best, providers were taking the pre-K standards for the Common Core and writing home-grown curriculum. At worst, providers were simply improvising activities for the youngsters to do during the school day. Funding was primarily cited as the key barrier, so the partnership set out to see what could be done. With the support of the local United Way, the action team received funding to begin rolling out a standard, research-based curriculum and assessment tool across early childhood providers in the city. Not only would the curriculum help providers to improve the quality of teaching and learning, but the accompanying assessment tool would help teachers to understand student-level development as children transition from infant and toddler settings to pre-K and through the transition to kindergarten. By standardizing the curriculum and assessment tool in use, the data follow the child, meaning that mobility no longer is a barrier to personalized instruction.

All along the way, the role of the action team has not been to create new programs or mandates. The team's role has been to bring together diverse partners, who each hold a tiny piece of the puzzle, and ensure that the best decisions for children are made. Due to the Albany Promise partnership, this kind of work continues to happen all across the cradle-to-career pipeline in Albany.

YOU CAN'T IMPROVE WHAT YOU CAN'T MEASURE

In many areas of Albany Promise's work, the complete lack of data about a specific outcome area was a large part of the reason why no efforts at improvement had been successful—either nothing had moved the dial, or no dial even existed. This staggering lack of understanding around the thousands of critical inputs that are required to, for example, help a third grade student to read at grade level, have caused educators and program providers to continue to invest and lead by hunches rather than by data. Traditionally, education outcomes are measured by lagging indicators—they typically are measured one to five years after any treatment has been applied. Imagine waiting one to five years to measure whether or not a jet engine for a commercial airliner was properly assembled, or waiting three to seven years to see if a major medical surgery was effective. We simply would not stand for those kinds of wait times, and yet we apply this outdated standard to education.

A significant body of work for Albany Promise came in the form of gradually building the data infrastructure necessary to establish better decision-making practices. This work was slow-moving and unsexy, but it was critically important for the partnership to show impact. The partnership knew that it was not in its best interest to grow its own data capacity but rather to connect to existing expertise on the needs of the partnership. This connection came in the form of partnership with the University at Albany's Center for Human Services Research (CHSR), an entity of the School of Social Welfare. With a team of highly trained data scientists on staff, CHSR was a perfect way for the university to contribute to the efforts of the partnership. Immediately, the team had capacity for and access to the types of data that the partnership needed to move the work forward. Additionally, researchers at CHSR were able to better tailor their work to the needs of the school district instead of taking on research agenda items that may not have practical applications for district leaders. Take, for example, a mobility study that was done by CHSR and had actionable implications for the district. Through the partnership, the analysis gathered found real-time application and further analysis. This kind of partnership is another place where the research needs of higher education and the real-time needs of collective impact partnerships are mutually beneficial to both parties.

[Building a data infrastructure] was slow-moving and unsexy, but it was critically important for the partnership to show impact.

A NEW KIND OF LEADERSHIP

Leadership plays no small role in any collective impact strategy—in fact, in many cases, it can be the critical catalyst to get a partnership started and sometimes the glue that holds an existing partnership together (Edmondson & Zimpher, 2014). But the type of leadership required is not the traditional kind of leadership we are accustomed to seeing and identifying and for which we train leaders. Instead, Lovegrove and Thomas (2013) outline triple-strength leadership and explain why it is so rare. Tri-sector leaders are people who can bridge the gaps and work fluidly between the business, government, and social spheres. Since the work of improving educational outcomes is at the intersection of these three important worlds, it is critical to the success of a partnership to find a leader who can move easily between each sector. These kinds of leaders have to balance competing motives, acquire transferable skills, develop contextual intelligence, forge intellectual threads, build integrated networks, and maintain a prepared mind. Research has shown that tri-sector leaders consistently deliver results when faced with difficult, multifaceted issues, which makes them an incredible resource for moving the work forward.

The leaders of Albany Promise have demonstrated tri-sector leadership talent, and a large part of the initiative's success can be attributed to their leadership skills. As the partnership developed, a sense of synergy emerged between the leaders. At no point was this dynamic clearer than during the launch of the *2014 Report Card* (The Albany Promise, 2014). The annual release to the community of data as measured against the outcome areas is a critically important part of maintaining accountability internally within the partnership as well as externally to the public.

During the launch event, as the leadership detailed the progress made in the preceding 12 months, the public was able to see this frictionlessness in action. Instead of having each traditional "owner" of the data deliver the news, the partnership instead chose nontraditional leaders to present the data. For example, instead of having an early childhood leader detail the progress made toward kindergarten readiness, the president and CEO of the area's largest credit union detailed the progress of three-, four-, and five-year-olds in the area. Similarly, the region's chamber of commerce CEO spoke about the progress being made toward third and fourth grade literacy and math proficiency. The mayor delivered an update about college access and enrollment.

This approach took many audience members by surprise, as they probably would not have bet that a bank CEO would be able to delve into the nuts and bolts of curriculum and assessment at a developmentally appropriate level for young children. Through this process, the initiative gained additional credibility, as it became evident that these high-level leaders were not just signing off on work happening in the community or reading someone else's talking points. Rather, they were getting their hands dirty in the weeds of how to improve educational outcomes for children. Additionally, it continued to build trust between the partners on the ground and high-level leaders, as it was for some the first time that leaders of such stature could articulate the importance of their work.

The leadership of key members in the community has kept the Promise partnership focused, on track, and committed to delivering results. The work that Zimpher, Jones, Vanden Wyngaard, and Sheehan have integrated into their day-to-day activities has been integral to the success of the partnership.

Since the value of these kinds of leaders is dramatically important to the success of partnerships like Albany Promise, more thought should be put into developing these kinds of leaders—another area where higher education can and should be taking a leading role. In the preparation of students for their chosen fields, specific emphasis should be placed on exposing students to these kinds of leadership skills and expanding their opportunities for engagement in tri-sector projects and issues. Tri-sector issues should be incorporated into the formal leadership programs traditionally offered at universities and should also be used as experiential learning opportunities. Universities should also consider the role they could play in enabling midcareer professionals to gain these critical skills.

ANCHORING THE PARTNERSHIP

When the work of the partnership began, much of the staff time, resources, and initial investment was made by Zimpher, who had the experience to know that without some initial investment, the partnership would never take off. This initial investment led to some perceptions that the partnership was *her* initiative, that it was not broadly owned by the community. Once the work of the partnership began to take hold, it was critically important to overcome this perception, as even just the perception of its being owned by any single person or entity could damage the partnership and lead to factions and political maneuvering.

Once Jones took the reins as president at the University at Albany, it became clear that his institution was the best anchor entity for the work. A large presence in the city, coupled with Jones's dedication to this work, made it a perfect fit. In 2014, the backbone was officially transitioned to the University at Albany.

The functions of the backbone organization of a collective impact initiative include being a fiscal agent, housing the partnership physically, supporting fundraising and development, providing data support and analysis, convening the partnership, supporting policy advocacy, providing communication capacity, and providing staffing (see chapter 1). Each of these functions need not sit solely within one partner—in fact, it is encouraged that functions be shared so as to maintain neutrality among partners. For example, the University at Albany physically houses the partnership staff and acts as the fiscal agent, but another partner, the regional chamber of commerce, has lent its expertise in spearheading the fundraising efforts for the partnership. This arrangement enables both the university and the chamber to have stakes in the partnership's success.

The University at Albany has a unique opportunity to anchor the work being done by the partnership, as its tripartite mission of education, research, and service provides a solid foundation upon which to build. At the heart of the institution is the education of students. Many of the students who are currently in the K–12 pipeline will move into postsecondary education, and the university has a vested interest in insuring that as many students as possible are well prepared and interested in progressing to higher education. Moreover, colleges and universities have a responsibility for helping to strengthen the K–12 pipeline as they prepare the teachers who teach the students. The university's significant research portfolio in the areas of education, social work, and public policy mean that it has great depth of expertise to bring to the challenges that confront the city in which it resides. With new leadership, the university became focused on being a good neighbor in the community and a partner with the city. In fact, one of the four pillars that Jones established for his presidency was public engagement, and Albany Promise provided a pivotal framework for enabling the university to effectively realize this goal. This kind of explicit commitment through the formal tools of the institution, such as Jones's strategic pillars, enables the partnership to be less theoretical and more of a priority for action. As illustrated earlier, there were important touch points between the collective impact commitment and the three foundational tenets of the university's mission.

The connections of the partnership to higher education are numerous and ever-growing. As more higher education partners join the partnership, each brings to the table its own priorities and areas of interest, which all enrich the partnership. The work of the partnership also helps inform higher education of areas of need. For example, the work of the early childhood action team helped inform the local colleges of the need for a clearer degree-granting ladder for early childhood education providers. The need to build sustainable on-ramps to increase the quality and quantity of providers calls for deep cooperation between two- and four-year universities and public and private institutions. Without these specific calls to action, it can sometimes be difficult for competing institutions to work together.

As the partnership's work increases and impact deepens, we are starting to see a new narrative developing for Albany, one in which residents—either new or old—know that the success of their children is being paid close attention to by all stakeholders of this city.

THE PATH FORWARD

The work in Albany is far from over—in fact, it has just begun—but the strong relationships and infrastructure that Albany Promise has built provide a solid foundation for large-scale change. As the partnership has evolved, the needs and crises facing the educational landscape of the city have also evolved, bringing new areas of priority and urgency. A seemingly immeasurable part of collective impact work is the effect that the process has on each individual institution. Anecdotally we have seen individuals bring the data-driven, collective impact lens to their respective institutions. It is incredibly inspiring to see the members of this collaborative begin to bring their newly forged skills to impact the issues they face daily at their home institutions. Since collective impact is not about any one person or any singular leader, this organic growth of the lens around improvement is critical to reaching the partnership's goals.

As the partnership's work increases and impact deepens, we are starting to see a new narrative developing for Albany, one in which residents—either new or old—know that the success of their children is being paid close attention to by all stakeholders of this city. They know that the children's success is our collective success, and we will not stop until all our children succeed.

LESSONS LEARNED

Embrace process. The secret sauce is in the process—which can feel irrelevant to partners, but without it, partners will continue doing what they've always done.

Grow capacity. The backbone staff can't do the work, the partners must do the heavy lifting. To do this, they'll need to grow their own capacity to collect and analyze data and understand collective impact.

It's about leadership, just as much as it isn't. Strong, committed leaders can help move the work forward and keep people at the table, but without on-the-ground providers, teachers, and staff, practices won't change and outcomes won't move.

Stop trying to boil the ocean. Instead of taking on a dozen outcome areas or projects, choose a few, dig in, and deliver results. Capacity will come, but credibility is harder to come by.

Build trust. This work is fundamentally about changing behaviors of other humans. Build relationships, build trust, and be kind to one another. Accountability doesn't have to mean finger-pointing.

REFERENCES

The Albany Promise. (2014). *2014 report card.* Retrieved from http://www.albany.edu/news/files/ReportCard_2014-2.pdf

Edmondson, J., & Zimpher, N. L. (2014). *Striving together: Early lessons from achieving collective impact in education.* Albany: State University of New York Press.

Grondahl, P. (2007). *Mayor Corning: Albany icon, Albany enigma.* Albany, NY: State University of New York Press.

Lovegrove, N., & Thomas, M. (2013, September). Triple-strength leadership. *Harvard Business Review.* Retrieved from https://hbr.org/2013/09/triple-strength-leadership

Shonkoff, J. P., & Phillips, D. A. (2000). *From neurons to neighborhoods: The science of early childhood development.* Washington, DC: National Academy of Sciences Press.

Tuckman, B. (1965). Developmental sequence in small groups. *Psychological Bulletin 63*, 384–399. doi:10.1037/h0022100

U.S. Department of Education. (2015). *Programs: Promise neighborhoods.* Retrieved from http://www2.ed.gov/programs/promiseneighborhoods/index.html

7

WHAT LARGE-SCALE CHANGE LOOKS LIKE AND HOW TO GET THERE

Theories of Action

A CONVERSATION WITH JEFF EDMONDSON, JASON HELGERSON, DANETTE HOWARD, JAMES KVAAL, BECKY KANIS MARGIOTTA, AND JOE MCCANNON

MODERATED BY DAVID LEONHARDT

ABSTRACT

Large-scale change can be messy—but meaningful. The contributors to this chapter, each experts in collective impact, provide meaningful insights into their own work, the challenges in facilitating large-scale change, and how collective impact can be applied to addressing challenges facing higher education.

It is a fascinating time for higher education. On the one hand, it is quite clear that higher education is worth it. A college degree is worth it. The gap between what college graduates are making

---

This chapter is based on a panel discussion at the SUNY Critical Issues in Higher Education conference in 2014, on which this book is based. The discussion has been adapted to fit the format of this volume, and some parts have been omitted due to space constraints.

and what everyone else is making is at a record high. So, David Leonhardt asserts, one should look skeptically at all the "Is a college degree worth it?" talk.

As Leonhardt says, the only time people ask that question is on behalf of other people's kids. No one questions that it is worth it for their own children. The issue is not just money, either. It concerns the odds of being employed. It concerns health, happiness, and marriage. There are a myriad of contributions that education appears to make to one's overall well-being beyond the size of his or her paycheck.

And yet, clearly, Leonhardt observes, education also has a lot of challenges and even problems. The dropout rate at many colleges is extremely high, sometimes crossing 50%. There are funding challenges. There is enormous variation in quality, and there is not always a lot of accountability. And a whole new world of online learning creates both opportunities and also challenges.

The main focus of this panel discussion was to address the following question: How does higher education take small successes and make them big? In many realms—education, health care, technology—we see things that work small, but when they try to go big, they do not work, either because of execution or because of the population that they are trying to serve. That is, we often know how to do something right with a hundred people, but that strategy might not work for a thousand or a million people.

This difficulty is one of the most important issues that affects people's lives today. To address it, this panel included individuals with diverse expertise in the areas of education, health care, and technology. All the panelists applied their broad expertise to education, using what they have learned in their respective fields to inform the challenges that education faces. Each panelist drew on his or her experience to address the question of how to take something small and make it big—without running into the pitfalls. Their presentations were followed by a free-ranging conversation.

The first panelist was Jason Helgerson, Medicaid director for New York State. He leads New York Governor Andrew Cuomo's efforts to increase quality and reduce cost growth in the area of health care. Before coming to New York, he was in Wisconsin, helping to implement BadgerCare Plus, which allowed the state to achieve the goal of having 98% of Wisconsinites with health insurance coverage. This program was, in many ways, a forerunner to the Affordable Care Act.

Next was Jeff Edmondson, who is the managing director of StriveTogether. StriveTogether works on cradle-to-career initiatives, trying to expand successful programs to reach larger groups. When you see a program that works, such as a preschool, how do you make it big? Edmondson is based in Cincinnati, and he works in communities in Cincinnati and Northern Kentucky, as well as around the country.

The third panelist was James Kvaal, deputy director of the Domestic Policy Council at the White House. He served as the policy director of President Barack Obama's 2012 reelection campaign. He has been a deputy undersecretary of the U.S. Department of Education and a special assistant to the president in the White House.

The fourth panelist was Danette Howard, vice president of the Lumina Foundation. Lumina's goal is to help 60% of Americans between the ages of 25 and 64 to achieve a four-year degree, a two-year degree, a professional certificate, or another credential by 2025. Before coming to Lumina, Howard was Maryland's secretary of higher education. In addition to having been a researcher at the University of Maryland, College Park, she worked directly with students and others at the University of Maryland, Baltimore County.

Becky Margiotta was the fifth panelist. She and Joe McCannon, the sixth panelist, co-founded the Billions Institute. They are trying to determine how to solve the world's biggest problems using the billions of people around the world. Margiotta just completed the very successful 100,000 Homes Campaign, which is building homes for the most vulnerable homeless people. Margiotta has degrees from both West Point and The New School.

McCannon is former senior advisor at the Centers for Medicare and Medicaid Services. Previously, he was vice president at the Institute for Health Care Improvement, which has been one of the most interesting places in the country to think about this issue of scale, trying to figure out how to ensure that entirely preventable errors that kill people in hospitals and elsewhere are avoided.

What follows is the panelists' discussion of how we can go from small successes to big successes without repeating the failures that many well-intentioned places experience.

JASON HELGERSON ON MEDICAID REDESIGN: FOUR STEPS TO SUCCESS

Big system change is hard, but I believe—and my experience indicates—that big change is, in fact, possible. In my view, there are four core elements that lead to success.

First and foremost, you need a very clear vision, a very clear goal in terms of what you are trying to achieve. Without that, change can be a significant challenge. Moreover, if you do not set the right mission and the right goal, it can confuse your stakeholders and make it difficult.

Second, you need to build and maintain momentum. Here is where, to be successful, you often need to break the objective into smaller component parts. My case, the case of Medicaid redesign in New York State, was very, very complicated. Medicaid is the largest government program in the state—a $57-billion-a-year enterprise with about 6 million participants. It constitutes a third to almost 40% of the total state budget. The goal of New York's Medicaid redesign was to try to make financially sustainable a program that was not sustainable, growing at 13% a year.

Instead of using a-one-size-fits-all or single-bullet approach to achieve this goal, we tried to break the problem into component parts and pursue many different reforms simultaneously. Each reform was realized in its own unique time frame. Over a five-year period, 235 distinct initiatives were implemented. The goal was to show immediate successes, build off those successes, and build a sense of momentum in which the broader community of stakeholders would believe. I am a big believer in building and maintaining momentum to be successful.

Stakeholders' engagement needs to be managed in ways that lead to their actually seeing themselves in the final product. They need to feel like they are part of it—that the invitation to be involved was more than lip service.

The third core element is stakeholder engagement, which we, under Governor Andrew Cuomo's leadership, have tried to practice. In the past, governors would propose changes to giant government programs behind closed doors, or they would announce them in the state budget proposal. There would be the inevitable political quarrelling, and most of the time, the issue just got kicked down the path, with very little actual progress.

In light of this history, what Governor Cuomo tried to do for Medicaid redesign was bring those interests together and charge them with coming up with a plan, incorporating their ideas in meaningful ways and building consensus. This approach is not easy, but I'm a big believer that it can be achieved, especially if you complete the fourth and final piece of the process, which is process itself.

I think that it is sometimes misunderstood, or folks take it for granted, that you need to manage this process. Stakeholders' engagement needs to be managed in ways that lead to their actually seeing themselves in the final product. They need to feel like they are part of it—that the invitation to be involved was more than lip service.

This approach is sometimes hard because it means yielding power and authority. It also means yielding the center stage in terms of design, policy solutions, and implementation strategies. But when you use this approach and get stakeholders to buy in and actually see themselves in the initiative, it can be very, very powerful.

In New York State, we have reduced per-recipient Medicaid spending to 2003 levels. I think that, when we started this endeavor, no one would have thought that achievement was possible, given the program's track record and path at the time. But I am a big believer—particularly if you break a change process into its component parts, engage stakeholders, and build and maintain momentum—you can be successful.

JEFF EDMONDSON: THREE PRIORITIES FOR SYSTEMS CHANGE

My organization, StriveTogether, was featured in a *Stanford Social Innovation Review* article on collective impact (Kania & Kramer, 2011) that made it sound like big systems change was super easy. It is wonderful that they were able to boil down collective impact and make it seem like anybody could achieve big systems change—let's just wake up and hold hands and sing "Kumbaya," and all of a sudden, we are going to change the system. But it is just not that easy. In Cincinnati and Northern Kentucky, the location of StriveTogether's founding partnership, we like to say that the article is a sanitized version of reality.

StriveTogether works every day to change six big outcomes: kindergarten readiness, early grade reading, middle grade math, high school graduation, college entrance, and college completion. To improve these outcomes, we have brought together all the stakeholders, and together we are making progress. We are seeing incredible improvements in early grade reading and college going, not by starting new programs but by identifying what already works, but it is a struggle every single day.

In 2011 I had the opportunity to pass the work in Cincinnati to a colleague of mine and work to build a national network of communities using the Strive model (see chapter 4). Now we have a national network of 53 communities that are trying to learn—fail forward—from what we have done in Cincinnati. In these communities, we have begun to create the systems change of moving communities from talk to action.

StriveTogether has a theory of action that begins to break down this concept of collective impact into phases—early stage, middle stage, and late stage work—where we bring the partners together, get agreement on outcomes, and begin to use data in new and different ways to lift up what works and achieve better results.

We recently convened all 53 of the communities in our national network, the StriveTogether Cradle-to-Career Network. Participants lifted up three components of systems change on which we must focus if we want to realize systems change. These communities have been working on these three components to drive systems change over the last four or five years.

First, communities have to stop thinking only about collaboration in the collective and start thinking about the individual partner's role in change. One potential problem with how collective impact has come to be described is that everybody uses the collaboration frame, where they assume they can show up to a meeting once a month or once every other month and, all of a sudden, everything is going to change. The truth of the matter is, for systems change to happen, each individual in the room, each individual in a partnership, has to behave differently every day. That is, everybody has to look in the mirror and say, "What am I doing right now that's contributing to the fact that too many kids are not successful in preschool or that too many kids are not ready to graduate from college. What am I doing every single day?"

Second, we have to focus on the most vulnerable students and equity issues. If we do not address the needs of those who are struggling the most and be honest about the equity issues that they face, we will not get people to believe that we can change systems.

The third piece, which is the lever for the first two, is that we have to use data as often as possible—hopefully every day—to identify the bright spots to lift up what works and ask people, "Can you change what you're doing every day? Can you change what you're doing right now to make sure that we're scaling what works for kids?

StriveTogether has a theory of action that begins to break down this concept of collective impact into phases—early stage, middle stage, and late stage work—where we bring the partners together, get agreement on outcomes, and begin to use data in new and different ways to lift up what works and achieve better results.

Can you do that each and every day?" This approach forces people to question what they are doing right now rather than just admire the problem and say, "Oh, that's terrible. Oh, we're just doing terribly!"

We can then use the data and the bright spots to answer the question, "Can we do that for the most vulnerable children?" For example, we found out in Milwaukee that a certain type of attendance team, focused on getting kids to school, was working with families once a week and was successfully getting kids to school. Could this model be replicated in other places?

If you focus on changing your behavior every day—making sure that, without a doubt, people are focused on the most vulnerable and using data to do both of those things consistently over time—our sense is that you can accomplish systems change.

JAMES KVAAL: SYSTEMS CHANGE IN HIGHER EDUCATION

This work is so central to where President Obama thinks our country needs to go. He said that if his first term was about the need to end two wars overseas and to deal with the worst economic crisis since the Great Depression, the second term should focus on another problem that is equally large: the stagnation of middle-class living standards over the last couple decades.

It is obviously a complicated problem with a lot of potential solutions to it. It is hard, however, to imagine any meaningful effort to progress on that problem without increasing educational attainment, without helping more people earn college degrees. That's the thinking behind the goal that he set to have the United States regain its status as having the highest proportion of college graduates in the world by 2020.

A generation ago, the United States led the world in educational attainment. Our older workers today are still more likely to have a college degree than their peers in any other country. But if you look at younger workers, we are now eleventh. The reason for this drop is because, over the past generation, we have essentially stood still while other countries have passed us by.

When we began working on the higher education policy speech that the president gave at SUNY about a year ago, we were asking many of these same questions: What is it that people are doing well that we can replicate? How do we build on what we know? What can we learn from health care?

Isolated programs exist in which people are helping students from the most disadvantaged backgrounds succeed. They are helping students to learn much more, faster, and they are finding newer and less expensive ways to teach. I think what we as a community are not doing as well is identifying where these strategies are working, especially if the location is someplace other than where we are. We are also struggling to figure out how to replicate these programs—or better yet, how to improve upon them.

We are trying to pursue some strategies in higher education that are similar to some of the techniques that are working in health care. For example, we must be honest and transparent about the state of higher education. To that end, we have put up the College Scorecard[1] to help students and parents get easy access to the most important indicators about how colleges and universities are doing.

We are working now to improve College Scorecard data to have better, standardized measures in such areas as graduation rates and employment outcomes, for example.

Beyond making these data accessible, we are building evidence of what works and how we know what works better. The Department of Education's Investing in Innovation Fund (i3),[2] for example, has been very influential in our thinking, at least in our own hallways. The thesis there is that we want to let the money follow the evidence, and we want to build the evidence. I3 is structured with three evidence tiers. If you have an idea that is promising but docs not have a lot of evidence behind it, you are given money to try it out and test it. If you have an idea that seems to work but has only moderate evidence behind it, you are given funding to replicate the idea, evaluate it, and demonstrate that it works. If you have an innovation with really strong evidence behind it, then you are given an even larger grant to expand or replicate it.

I3's emphasis on evidence is really important for two reasons. First, it allows us to demonstrate that funding is following results, and we are really making hardheaded, pragmatic decisions regarding the use of federal dollars. Second, it changes the incentive structure for the entire field. When people are writing grant applications for the first time, in developing those plans, they are going to the Department of Education's What Works Clearinghouse[3] to look at the research evidence. They are trying to figure out how to design an evidence-based proposal that will build on existing evidence. They are trying to determine what can be learned from their project to give back and pay it forward—to make sure that they are continuing to build the research pool.

> Isolated programs exist in which people are helping students from the most disadvantaged backgrounds succeed. What we as a community are not doing as well is identifying where these strategies are working, . . . figure[ing] out how to replicate these programs, and . . . how to improve upon them.

So we are approaching higher education reform with honesty and evidence. The third aspect—one thing that we have yet to mention today—is resources. The work of the Institute for

Healthcare Improvement to keep healthcare costs at low levels has been incredibly influential. Important factors limiting these expenses to historically low levels the last couple of years have been the reforms in the Affordable Care Act (ACA) and the incentives that the ACA gives our healthcare system to integrate care to focus not on the number of treatments the patient gets but how healthy someone is, to tackle some of the low-hanging fruit.

In higher education, we should be thinking about how the vast majority of funding goes to institutions on the basis of initial enrollment. What kind of impact does that policy have at a campus level if an administrator has a good idea that costs a little more but helps increase completion rates? Funding to encourage completion has to come out of other funding streams because there are no dedicated resources to reward higher completion rates or more learning.

DANETTE HOWARD: THE ROLE OF SCALING IN SYSTEMS CHANGE

At this conference we are talking about big, hairy, audacious goals, and the Lumina Foundation certainly has one of those: 60% of Americans with high-quality postsecondary degrees or other credentials by 2025. The good news is college attainment is increasing, so if you look at our baseline from when we started measuring in 2009, there has certainly been an uptake, but it is not increasing fast enough. We are still about 34 million degrees short of where we need to be to meet that 2025 goal. If we continue to increase graduates at the current pace, we will still be about 19 million short in 2025, so to meet our goal, system change certainly has to happen.

We have talked about applying "systemness" to higher education, and I also want to discuss a similar term, "scalability," because Lumina here at this conference is really focused on which approaches, strategies, and interventions were designed for scale. Not all strategies are actually scalable.

At the Lumina Foundation, we have made some investments in higher education that have produced excellent results, but they have cost millions of dollars and have impacted very few students. Now we are much more focused on those interventions that are going to reach the millions of students whom we really need to be serving. Our practices and our investments are based on those interventions that we know will work.

We invest our resources in initiatives that are data-based and can be supported by evidence, such as transforming developmental and remedial education. I personally do not think that a student should sit in a remedial course for three or four semesters. When I was in Maryland, the data were very clear that too many of our students begin and end their college careers in developmental and remedial education. We are certainly focused on scaling changes in that area, looking at better pathways that will get students through more quickly to a degree.

Institutions' mining their own data is a big part of identifying these pathways. One of the best but also most sobering experiences that I had in Maryland was when we looked at all our community colleges across the continuum to see how many credits students had when they finally earned an associate's degree. The total ranged from 67 credits at one community college to 116 at another. No one can tell me that there is not a problem there.

Now we are much more focused on those interventions that are going to reach the millions of students whom we really need to be serving. Our practices and our investments are based on those interventions that we know will work.

Scaling also has to do with policy. We were able to use those data as a baseline and argue that we needed a policy to make sure that students are not actually only four credits shy of a bachelor's degree when they get an associate's degree. I think we need to also consider institutional policy, system-wide policies, and even state policies and the role that they can play in scale.

At Lumina, we are in a really unique position to give institutions some room to take risks that they otherwise would not be able to take. When I was at an institution, I was very grateful for the support of external foundations because, without those initial funding sources, we would not have been able to try new and innovative things and to take risks.

We at Lumina really hope that we can be a partner with higher education institutions in thinking about how to bring to scale some of these approaches and strategies that we know work. We also hope that the collaboration will not stop there, that you can use some of the funding that we might provide to leverage additional funding. The best stories are those that I hear when a representative of a college or university or system says, "You gave us $1 million, but then the state saw the great work that we were doing, and they supported us to the tune of $50 million." That is one way in which scale at the system level is achieved.

Finally, we have to talk about sustainability. If an organization like Lumina gives you $2 million, but after the funding is gone the work ends, that is not long-term change. Nor is it sustainable change. It also is not taking success to scale. Enough has been done over the last several years that we know what works. We know what can be scaled, and we know what leads to sustainable change.

BECKY MARGIOTTA: DISRUPTIVE INNOVATION

I would like to share with you a story about chronic street homelessness and how it really relates, I think, to what we want to do in education.

Back in 2003, I was hired to reduce street homelessness in Times Square by two-thirds in three years. In fact, my office was on 43rd and 8th in the Times Square Hotel, and at the time 55 people were sleeping outside on a night when it would be about 18 degrees in the middle of winter. It was the highest density of street homelessness in New York City.

I had just come out of the military, and I knew absolutely nothing about homelessness whatsoever. The most frequent question that I was asked was, "Who put you in charge?" And I responded, "I did," which is a key distinction between working within a small-scale change and then large-scale change.

My team turned the way that street outreach was done on its head, and we did it by focusing on the most vulnerable people who had been out there on the streets for decades in many cases—people whom other outreach teams walked past and assumed were service-resistant and did not want help. We worked on helping those people get directly into housing, which was a very disruptive innovation.

The people to whom we reached out could have included someone with severe mental illness who also had a substance abuse issue, whose foot is falling off because of diabetes, and who is living in his or her own feces and talking to himself or herself. When everybody walks past this person, they just look the other way. By working with these individuals, we reduced street homelessness by 87% in four years. We got it down to where it was just one person, and the *New York Times* wrote a story about him, like, "Oh, my God, who is this guy?" And he is in housing now, too.

We had a very successful pilot. After that, I spent two years going from city to city, with the hubris of replication, and I quickly learned that the questions to ask were: What are the adaptable ideas? What are the spreadable ideas within this street-to-home model? For two years I lived on the road, helping communities adapt this model.

A call from Louisville, Kentucky, was my Waterloo. I thought, "I'm not going to a community that has, like, 29 homeless people. With the money you'd pay me as a consultant, you could house everyone on your streets, right?"

It was then that I decided that, instead of my just responding to whoever calls to help them with this one model that had been very successful, what I would really like to do is house 100,000 people straight off the streets, people exactly like those I just described. So in 2010 we launched the 100,000 Homes Campaign. It was a national movement to find and house 100,000 of the most long-term homeless and vulnerable people straight off the streets of America. Long story short, we did large-scale change development.

We enrolled 186 cities. First, we presented very stark pictures, before-and-after pictures of people housed. The difference is stunning. Second, we encouraged communities to get to the level where they were housing at a rate at which they would end homelessness. If a community were housing 2.5% more of its homeless members every month, they were on track to eliminate homelessness. They were admitted to the 2.5 Percent Club, which allowed an identity shift: They were one of us now.

When we started this club, no communities were housing at 2.5% per month. When we finished the campaign, 60 communities in America were housing at that rate, and they achieved the goal because we were constantly spreading the interventions that worked.

The sad news about homelessness is no one agency can achieve this goal on its own. It requires everyone to work together. Over the course of the campaign, we helped dozens of communities to

The sad news about homelessness is no one agency can achieve this goal on its own. It requires everyone to work together.

quadruple the rate at which they were housing their most vulnerable people. The 100,000 Homes experience provided lots of lessons on large-scale change that Joe and I are now channeling into the Billions Institute.

JOE MCCANNON: THE PROBLEM OF GIVING UP CONTROL

When I think of the core challenge in expansion or scaling, going from something that happens within an organization to something that impacts many organizations and many groups, it has to do with control. You have less control. You do not have executive authority to tell others, "You must do the following things."

Persuasion and influence become much more important. That was certainly true in the 100,000 Lives Campaign, the initiative to reduce harm in hospitals. To address that problem of control, we came up with three ideas or three principles that were very important to us—ways to engage people without having that executive authority.

First, we applied many stimulants. What I mean by that is to find a way to use every single method, every single tool, at your disposal to engage people. That can mean regulation. It can mean policy. It can mean recognition. It can mean celebration. It can mean collaboration.

There are all kinds of reasons why people would be drawn to do work. There are positive levers and there are negative levers. But the work of someone who is orchestrating large-scale change is to become a master at applying all these different levers very opportunistically. Whenever the opportunity arises, you have to be fast enough to seize the opportunity and take advantage of it.

The second idea has to do with what we call "wasting no will." People come to the work that they do on a daily basis with their own strong beliefs and their own strong desires, and rather than saying, "Here is our thing, and this is what we want you to do," we got good at saying, "Tell me what is important to you, or tell me about the bad experience you have had with medication in your hospital, or tell me about the worst thing that you have ever observed, and tell me what you want to do. Tell me what is really, really important to you."

Our answer to whatever people wanted to do was always, "Yes." So if a parent of a child who had been harmed in the course of care came to us and said, "You know, we are really worried about medication error. We want to work on that, and we want to start to make art about that in the lobby of the hospital," we said "Yes, absolutely." If a doctor came to us and said, "I want to work on central line infections," there was a place for that.

It came to a point where pharmaceutical company representatives were knocking on our door and saying, "We want to be part of your initiative." We were a little hesitant But we found a place for them. We had to find a place for everyone who wanted to contribute because doing this work takes so much energy and so many individuals' effort that you cannot waste any of the energy that people bring to the table.

> **[T]he core challenge in expansion or scaling, going from something that happens within an organization to something that impacts many organizations and many groups, . . . you have less control. . . . Persuasion and influence become much more important.**

The third idea, on which we leaned really heavily in the course of the work, was the idea of "getting to field." Getting to field means, "Let's not sit in our central office and pontificate and strategize and build the perfect plan. Let's get out to the field." It is like what Jeff Edmondson was saying, "Let's do the work every single day. Let's collect data on the progress we are making, and let's try new things every single day." Things like rate of testing and rate of learning became much more important to us than coming up with the perfect strategy or the perfect plan.

We stole a phrase from the U.S. Army: "Amateurs discuss strategy. Professionals discuss logistics." That idea sums up the heart of, I think, a large-scale initiative that works. We move from contemplation, which is actually kind of self-indulgent, to action, and we do our learning on the go.

THE IMPORTANCE OF DATA

Following the panelists' remarks, Leonhardt noted that many panelists talked about the importance of data. In some ways, he observed, there is nothing magical about data—it is just an accumulation of facts. But, he averred, there is a fair amount of resistance in many places to using data too much. This panel coincided with game seven of the 2014 World Series. Leonhardt recounted that general managers in baseball who have tried to push to use more data always feel a need to say, "Well, of course we don't just use data. Of course we use intuition as well."

In another anecdote about using data, Leonhardt shared that he was once sitting in a meeting with one of the top-performing hospital chains in the country, Intermountain Health Care in Utah, at a great moment in which hospital executives were reviewing the case of a doctor who was inducing too many babies too early. The doctor was not in the room, but they were talking about his case. The person leading the discussion said, "Well, we all know what the first response is," and the whole room said, "The data are wrong, right?"

Leonhardt invited the panelists to respond to the question, "How do you bring people along to be willing to look at data, even when it is not showing what they might believe about themselves?"

Jeff Edmondson of StriveTogether responded first. "In Cincinnati," he explained,

> we had a key moment. Nancy Zimpher was president of the University of Cincinnati at the time, and we were trying to figure out how we could get to systems change. We were trying to put out a report card, a baseline report card on where we stood on the six outcomes that I listed. There were incredible fights among all the different stakeholders. It was akin to the fights that happen in the literacy world around phonics versus whatever the other side is when it literally feels like a war is going on. It was actually the president of the other university in town, Northern Kentucky University, with whom Nancy Zimpher worked very closely, who stood up and said, "Folks, we cannot let perfect be

the enemy of good. We cannot let perfect be the enemy of good. We have to put out the data we have and trust that over time good data will drive out bad data. Not even in the private sector do you have perfect data to make incredibly important decisions. You have the data you have, and you need to work with that data right now and make the best use of it that you possibly can."

I think that higher education has a huge role to play here because to have a university president say that, and to have some deans of the college of education say, "We can't let perfect be the enemy of good," was a big deal because a lot of the university counterparts were saying that we needed perfect data. That is, we needed to have data at the level of a double-blind randomized controlled trial to do anything whatsoever.

I think what we have to be comfortable with is that, yes, there is a role for research and evaluation as it has been defined, but there is just as important a role—maybe over time a more important role—for using data for continuous improvement each and every day. So I have to, knowing that there are many higher education leaders here, put back one of the things that I think you all could do every single day. Ask, "That's great that we need this high standard for using data to get to the evidence that's being really pushed by the administration. Can we think about how to use data every single day to make improvements?"

Danette Howard of the Lumina Foundation continued the discussion: I can talk about the higher education context because in Maryland there was a real concern that people would interpret the data incorrectly, or use the data out of context, or see one data point and make an irrational decision that would have a negative impact on a campus. And a couple of things happened. We had leadership from the governor, who said repeatedly, "What gets measured gets done." So there was an

We cannot let perfect be the enemy of good. We have to put out the data we have and trust that over time good data will drive out bad data.

expectation that we were going to take a hard look at the data.

The data might reveal some things with which we were not pleased, but at least we would know where to target our energy and resources. We also tried to present a picture of how the data could be used to the advantage of the institutions. Even if you were an institution where the students were graduating with 116 credits for an associate's degree when they could have been graduating—and should have been graduating—with 60 or 62 credits, once you knew that, what, then, would you do?

That particular campus president immediately went back, conducted degree audits, and saw that there were hundreds of students who could graduate right then and there. Not only did she graduate those students, but she put the policy in place that such credit accumulation would never happen again.

It is crucial to let folks know that, while data can be used for evil, it really should be used for good. And we must give them clear examples of how it can be used for good, not only for the benefit of the institutions but ultimately for the students whom we all serve.

The Billions Institute's Becky Margiotta shared her experience as well: The 100,000 Homes Campaign was in a similar situation to Lumina's circumstance with its 2025 goal: Based on current trends, Lumina is going to be a couple million students short. With a year and a half left in the campaign, our projections were that we were going to be 70,000 homes short.

When we hit 10,000, I had already gotten a tattoo of "100,00"—with a comma in the wrong place and a holding place for where that last zero would be when the 100,000th person got housed. So I did that—perhaps a moment of excessive exuberance.

So when my data person said, "Becky, you're on track to be the 30,000 Homes Campaign," I thought, "That is really bad." We had that moment. We faced the data, and from that point on, every single week, the first thing we did in our team meeting was face the data on how many communities we had enrolled and their performance.

What we had to do was get hundreds of cities, when all we had was good looks and personality, to improve the rate at which they were housing the most dirty, stinky, vulnerable homeless people on the planet from 1.6% per month to an average of 2.5% per month. The way we did it was to create—and this had never been done before, which is somewhat shocking—a report for the communities in which we reported the current rate at which they said they were housing these people and all of the resources that have been squirreled away in a variety of different hiding places across multiple organizations.

The report also indicated the rate at which the communities would need to house people to be making any progress whatsoever—to hit the 100,000 shared goal. We presented these data, and what we had to do to achieve this goal was help people to overcome their fear.

It is crucial to let folks know that, while data can be used for evil, it really should be used for good. And we must give them clear examples of how it can be used for good, not only to the benefit of the institutions but ultimately for the students whom we all serve.

Joe and I talk a lot about creating a container that is free of fear, and that is an important role of leaders. So we started sessions in which we discussed these reports with me standing up and saying, "These are the five ways you are going to get scared. You are going to fight me; you are going to run away; you are going to faint; and you are going to be looking at your Blackberry, not paying any attention, or you're going to freeze. This is what it is going to look like, and that's okay. This is going to happen. But we're going to look at the data together." I needed to hold up the mirror, and show people what the current situation looks like, and remind everyone that we were going to do this together. It was routine for communities to cry. We called them "tears of change." We had Kleenex on the tables and told them that it's okay to shed a tear. So that is what leaders do: They create a context within which you reduce the fear enough, but you have enough data that you can support people making different decisions.

Those communities that went through this process together quadrupled their housing placement rates in 100 days, by the way. I'm talking days, not years.

Jeff Edmondson interjected:

I want to quote Becky really quickly and make sure I get it right. We had a conversation, a quick conversation on the phone once, and I asked, "How did you get people to be willing to talk to each other about data?" Becky's answer was, "Well, I hired people that the folks in the community actually liked." Becky Margiotta confirmed that was her strategy. Edmondson continued by sharing that it was really interesting, because we often think technically, and we want to get technical around data. But you need to have people who can break down the data so that people can actually hear it and trust that it is not going to be used as a hammer but as a flashlight to help them do what they are doing better. I think there is something in that because when we think about data, we get this picture of a data geek, a wonk, in our head. We actually just need people whom folks like and trust with that data to present it to them.

[Leaders] create a context within which you reduce the fear enough, but you have enough data that you can support people making different decisions.

Becky Margiotta responded to Jeff Edmondson, "I think one of my greatest assets as a leader of this movement was that I was likable. Data are used so often as a punishment, and you have to create a shame-free environment to pull this stuff off."

Jason Helgerson of the New York State Medicaid Redesign Team continued:

I am a big believer in the idea that you need data to convince people that the status quo is not sustainable. If people, by their nature, believe in and are comfortable with the status quo, even if they acknowledge there are problems with it, they will want to defend it. It is a natural human reaction to try to keep things where they are because there is always that fear of the unknown. If you want to convince people that change must occur, you must use data to show that."

It is not only that you show the problem, but I think that if you can show that the status quo is not only unsustainable but immoral, you potentially create a very powerful incentive for change that I think is underappreciated. Sometimes we put these statistics out there, and we do not talk about the fact that these are statistics that are real human beings.

I think that healthcare is a perfect example. We have a healthcare safety net in parts of the United States where the healthcare delivery system relies on the fact that people are getting sicker than they should have and are going into hospitals when they should not be there. That is what generates enough revenue to keep these institutions alive and functioning and people employed. And that, in my view, is immoral. We as a nation need to change that fundamental structure so that the providers survive when they are successful—not when people get sick, but when they get healthy.

In terms of our initial efforts to make Medicaid more sustainable, what we are doing now is trying to make the delivery system more cost-effective and refocusing the delivery system on trying to keep people well, as opposed to trying to maintain a system that is dependent on people getting sick and generating revenue and sustainability. This step is really, really hard. It is hard to get people who run these large institutions to understand that the system that empowers them, employs them, is, in essence, in my view, morally bankrupt. That is a challenge because it is very scary. They are used to a philosophy of filling beds.

"Heads and beds" is literally the phrase that is used across the industry, and it has to change, because if we are going to remove healthcare from its place as a sixth of our economy—we have to break away from that philosophy. And that is not easy.

I think that at the end of the day, people are motivated by a moral mission. I think that if you can communicate that mission to people, along with all your good statistics about why you need to improve and how you need to improve, I think you will be more successful at major system change.

THE ROLE OF STUDENTS IN LARGE-SCALE CHANGE

David Leonhardt's next question concerned the role that students should have in large-scale change. More bluntly, he asked: "Are expectations for students too low in higher education? Should we, for example, increase the incentives—both carrots and sticks—for behaviors such as remaining on pace to graduate in four or five years?" He noted that West Virginia offers a scholarship for which students can qualify by staying on track to graduate in four years. Upon providing this scholarship, the state saw a change in the number of kids who graduated in four years. Should we be offering more opportunities like this incentive?

Jeff Edmondson of StriveTogether confirmed that colleges and universities should be providing these opportunities. Leonhardt offered a caveat: "These incentives should be offered if they work." He continued by asking: "What are some of the practices, either from the lessons you all have seen in your own fields or specifically from higher education, that we should think about to put some of the onus on students without, obviously, ignoring the fact that many of these students may have to work, they have kids to care for, they have parents to care for?"

James Kvaal of the White House discussed several ideas considered in the past. In his view:

what makes this issue difficult is the need to be mindful of the challenges disadvantaged students may face. For some students, it is not realistic to take a full-time course load. Some students do struggle. Our system of higher education is very "American" in the sense that we believe in second chances—or even third chances. We want to let people get back on track. And there are things that we can do to help them.

For example, we have proposed changing the federal Pell grant program to give institutions a bonus if they are graduating both a large share of their Pell students and a large number of Pell students. These incentives would help institutions to focus on getting Pell students not just in the door but also through the door.

It would be worth looking at the academic requirements of the Pell program. New York State has, as part of the state scholarship grant program, a concept called "failure to pursue," which expects students to at least complete their classes even if they do not pass them. They are expected to at least finish the term and earn a failing grade. Federal education law has no such policy. In fact, the academic progress requirements for federal grants are very weak. These expectations would be a place to consider reform as well.

Jeff Edmondson continued:

It depends on if we are thinking about the institution as it operates now or about the institution as it may need to operate in the future. I think that we are seeing a trend toward completely individualized education, so it is not about the institution's statistics anymore. Rather, it is about the individual student's success.

For example, what if you said that rather than use a student advising system through which students get 15 minutes with whoever is staffing the advisement desk at the institution at the beginning of the semester, you change advising completely to be a deep, one-on-one relationship with somebody who asks the student about his or her goals for success and discusses with him or her what the student may need in order to thrive? The needs of the student should drive how we organize their educational journey to make sure that they get to what they define as their goal and what we know is needed for success.

Jason Helgerson of the New York Medicaid Redesign Team added to this discussion: "I think if you look at healthcare, one of the buzzwords is 'patient-centered.' Everyone is talking about how we can design healthcare systems to be patient-centered—putting the patient at the center of a system that has historically been a provider-centered."

Leonhardt observed that this history is remarkable, and Helgerson responded:

> Crazy as it sounds, it is true. I think it is the same in education. I am not a higher education expert, but I have gone through higher education myself. Having sat in large rooms and been lectured to, it can be a dehumanizing experience. It is not very student-centered. It can be very faculty-centered, with the faculty at the center of the universe. I am not saying you can change that model overnight, but the thought can be more about how the student is at the center.
>
> I think that in the private sector, in government, we are all victims of this phenomenon where we do not attempt to get feedback from our stakeholders, our customers, our employees as effectively as possible. I believe that if we start to think about education in a more student-centric, as opposed to institution-centric or faculty-centric, manner, it might be a way to start.

Joe McCannon of the Billions Institute continued:

> If you really want to know about the healthcare for chronic disease, do not ask a primary care physician. Ask someone who has diabetes. Ask someone who has chronic heart disease. These people really, really understand what it is like to navigate the system in all its complexity, in all its intricacy. I think that any industry that is interested in changing itself needs to bring the same discipline to the process. What does the customer need and require? Let's get really serious about knowing and understanding those needs and getting to the field.
>
> To this issue about setting higher standards for students, I want to offer a little nuance. I do not want to make too

fine a point, but there are more and less sophisticated ways to measure progress. You can say to a student, "You need to get an 80 or you fail out," or you can say, "I'm interested in your rate of progress over time, against yourself." If improvement is really the goal, if what we are really interested in is how a student is actually progressing—as is the case in health care when we assess healthcare facilities—our concern is not just a measure of a single point in time. We are interested in improvement over time, which is viewed as a much more just way of doing assessment, because at least people can point to the fact that they may not be at the level of some world-class teaching hospital, but they are making a lot of progress against themselves over time. I think we can design measurement in more sophisticated ways to have more impact.

RISK-TAKING IN HIGHER EDUCATION

David Leonhardt then observed that higher education appears to be arguably the most stable large, important segment of our economy. The list of important universities in each state, in the country, has changed remarkably little over a very long period of time. That stability seems to have both advantages and disadvantages.

"I would be interested," Leonhardt said, "in the panelists' thoughts about how higher education can have more turnover, assuming that it would have some benefits. For example, Jeff Edmondson used the phrase 'fail forward,' in which you start something, it does not work, and you get rid of it. What is it that higher education can do," Leonhardt asked, "to make sure that it is willing to take risks and be okay with the fact that some of those risks are not going to work out, and maybe others are going to grow into something that maybe even displaces things that exist now because they are so successful?"

Danette Howard of the Lumina Foundation responded:

I think that higher education is going to have to change because the market is demanding it. Our goal is 60%, but it does not just mean 60% four-year degrees or 60% associate's degrees. It means 60% of Americans having a credential that will allow them to be successful in the workforce.

What we know is some people are getting the training and education that they need not from our higher education institutions but from their employers or from other entities in the community that are able to award credit. They then translate that learning into a job. So I am hopeful that higher education understands this trend. Students certainly understand it. They are going where they can get the learning and the training that they need to succeed. To remain competitive and meet the needs of today's consumers—today's students who are very diverse and varied in their needs and how they want to pursue their education—I think that higher education is going to adjust because there are other providers who are serving the needs of today's students.

Becky Margiotta of the Billions Institute continued:

I have a real concrete answer to that question, based on Christensen's (1997) *The Innovator's Dilemma*. Disruptive innovation is a commitment, as part of the institution, that X% of your budget be dedicated to innovation, discovery, and trying new things. He recommends, I think, that 4% of your budget go toward trying new things. The key is that you do it in a disciplined way—not by just winging it, seeing what happens, and mad scientist type of stuff. Instead, you have a disciplined way of trying new ideas and spreading new ideas throughout the campus, putting your money where your mouth is in that 4%. The other really critical part is to isolate that 4% from the rest of the culture. You have to isolate the innovators from business as usual and protect them so that they can be truly innovative and create new things.

Margiotta's colleague, Joe McCannon, built on her remarks:

When I look at healthcare and the change of quality in hospitals in particular, the major driver has been boards of directors and senior executives. When board members decide that the way to assess themselves is not with an annual report that looks at metrics from the past, instead choosing to sit down every quarter, even better, every month, to ask, "How many people have we harmed as a result of medications? How many people have we harmed as a result of infections? How many people have we harmed as a result of surgical complication?" That practice, for me, is part of a set of leadership habits.

I can look at the calendar and tell you whether this organization has the rhythm or the tempo to learn and improve. For me, it is a process of reengineering the day-to-day work of the institution to drive that behavior. That signal from boards and from executives is very powerful.

Jeff Edmondson of StriveTogether made another suggestion:

Maybe one of the most powerful levers from those boards could be to add incentives so that, for example, if the primary incentives now in higher education involve publishing and bringing in resources for projects, perhaps another incentive could be to move the dial on significant social issues in the community. What if you were able to get tenure because you contributed to improving early grade reading rates or college readiness rates or college completion rates?

We are witnessing one community where leaders have started to pull together K–12 superintendents and university presidents to ask whether the universities, the colleges of education specifically, give data back to the K–12 districts on how the teachers that they have prepared are performing in the classroom. What if through this process we uncovered that some of the colleges of education were doing a phenomenal job preparing math teachers? Or maybe just one college of education was succeeding in that area, and we ask it to address that segment of our work. That is, that college of education would drill down

I can look at the calendar and tell you whether this organization has the rhythm or the tempo to learn and improve.

on only preparing math teachers, and another institution zeros in on preparing teachers to teach kids how to read.

We began to see that there is some segmentation in higher education institutions because they are really good at particular things. They are focusing on things that they do well rather than assuming that every institution has to be all things to all people. Colleges and universities may practice segmentation based on moving local dials—an incentive that celebrates improving local lives as opposed to publishing resources, research, and bringing in grants.

James Kvaal of the White House observed that the *U.S. News & World Report* rankings judge institutions in part by how many students they turn away:

It measures instructional quality by the amount the institutions spend. These criteria are the exact wrong types of questions that we should be asking when we are trying to build a higher education system that takes all types of students, is affordable, and produces good results.

If you were to look at the higher education system with a different lens and asked, "Where are the students going?," you would see that the community college system, essentially built over the last two generations, now enrolls half the students. Meanwhile, Cal State is building whole new campuses. So I think the challenge is to focus on institutions and systems—and SUNY is one—that are doing a great job enrolling all types of students, being affordable, and getting results so that our conversation around higher education is centered around the institutions that will produce millions more graduates. In this way, we are talking about the central role that those institutions will play in our future.

NOTES

1. See https://www.whitehouse.gov/issues/education/higher-education/college-score-card.
2. See http://www2.ed.gov/programs/innovation/index.html?utm_source=rssutm_medium=rssutm_campaign=the-u-s-department-

of-education-announced-the-start-of-the-134-million-2014-investing-in-innovation-i3-grant-competition.
3. See http://ies.ed.gov/ncee/wwc/.

REFERENCES

Christensen, C. M. (1997). *The innovator's dilemma: When new technologies cause great firms to fail.* Boston, MA: Harvard Business School Press.
Kania, J., & Kramer, M. (2011, winter). Collective impact. *Stanford Social Innovation Review.* Retrieved May 15, 2015 from http://www.ssireview.org/articles/entry/collective_impact

Contributors

Carolyn Aiken is an associate principal in McKinsey & Company's Organization Practice based in the Toronto Office who has pioneered innovative approaches to CEO, top-team, and organization-wide change effectiveness.

B. Alex Finsel is a public high school economics and U.S. history teacher for North Colonie Central Schools in Latham, New York. He also serves as the district's summer school principal for grades 9–12. Previously, he served in the United States Marine Corps for ten years. Currently, Alex is a doctoral student in educational administration and policy studies at the University at Albany, State University of New York. His research interests include school building leadership, teacher evaluation, public education policy, and the economics of education. In 2011, Alex received an instructional technology grant from the New York State Association for Computers and Technologies in Education (NYSCATE) for Real-Time Data Collection, Analysis, and Decision Making Technology in Social Studies.

Jeff Edmondson is managing director of StriveTogether, a subsidiary of KnowledgeWorks. Prior to founding StriveTogether, Edmondson was the founding executive director of the Strive Partnership in Cincinnati and Northern Kentucky, a partnership of postsecondary, K–12, business, philanthropic, nonprofit, and civic organizations aimed at increasing education outcomes for students throughout the region. Strive Partnership is one of the most notable collective impact initiatives, and Edmondson has drawn on the work of the partnership to develop StriveTogether and the National Cradle-to-Career Network.

JONATHAN S. GAGLIARDI currently serves as the chancellor's fellow on Completion for the State University of New York (SUNY) System and as deputy director of the National Association of System Heads (NASH). In his role as chancellor's fellow, Dr. Gagliardi is helping to lead SUNY's efforts to increase degree completion across New York State. As deputy director of NASH, Dr. Gagliardi has guided the creation of new strategic priorities focused on student success and decision analytics, leveraging systems as a mechanism for innovation, diffusion, and scale. He is recognized for his expertise in innovation and entrepreneurship, serving as an advisory board member for the Association of Public and Land-grant Universities Commission on Innovation, Competitiveness, and Economic Prosperity. Dr. Gagliardi holds a PhD in higher education administration and policy, an MS in higher education administration and policy, and a BA in history and sociology from the University at Albany (SUNY).

JASON HELGERSON became New York's Medicaid director in January 2011. New York's Medicaid program provides vital healthcare services to over five million New Yorkers and has an annual budget in excess of $54 billion. Mr. Helgerson also serves as the executive director for New York's Medicaid Redesign Team. In this capacity he leads Governor Andrew Cuomo's effort to fundamentally reshape the state's Medicaid program in order to both lower costs and improve healthcare quality. Prior to arriving in New York, Mr. Helgerson was Wisconsin's Medicaid director. In that capacity, he administered the state's nationally recognized BadgerCare Plus program for children and families (Wisconsin's Family Medicaid, SCHIP, and Healthy Start Program), BadgerCare Plus Core Plan, SeniorCare (Pharmacy Plus waiver), FoodShare (Supplemental Nutrition Assistance Program), and Wisconsin's Chronic Disease Program.

DANETTE HOWARD is vice president for policy and mobilization at Lumina Foundation, the nation's largest private foundation focused solely on increasing student access and success in postsecondary education. Dr. Howard oversees several of Lumina's key strategies to increase Americans' attainment of high-quality postsecondary degrees and credentials, including strategic work in both state and federal policy and the foundation's growing national convening function. Prior to joining Lumina, Howard served as secretary of higher education in Maryland, leading the state's postsecondary education coordinating agency, the Maryland Higher Education Commission. A nationally regarded analyst and thought leader, Howard previously served as director of research and policy analysis at the Maryland Higher Education Commission. She also held positions as the assistant director of higher education policy at the Education Trust in Washington, D.C.; as a researcher at the University of Maryland, College Park; and as a student affairs administrator and admissions counselor at the University of Maryland, Baltimore County.

SCOTT KELLER is a partner in McKinsey & Company's Chicago office. He leads McKinsey's Organizational Behavior Practice in the Americas and has deep experience in counseling senior executives on organization performance and change effectiveness.

JAMES KVAAL is the deputy director of the Domestic Policy Council, which coordinates the domestic policy-making process in the White House. Prior to his current position, he was the policy director on the Obama for America 2012 campaign. In the first term of the Obama administration, he worked as deputy undersecretary at the U.S. Department of Education and special assistant to the president for economic policy, where he worked on higher education and labor market policies, including student financial aid, community college reform, and simplifying the student aid application. Kvaal previously served in positions in the House of Representatives, the Senate, and the Clinton White House. He graduated from Stanford University and Harvard Law School.

JASON E. LANE is vice provost for Academic Planning and Strategic Leadership and senior associate vice chancellor for the State University of New York, where he is responsible for the development and implementation of academic, economic, global, and leadership initiatives across the system. Dr. Lane is also an award-winning scholar and expert in the emerging relationship between higher education, policy and politics, and globalization. He has written more than 50 journal articles, book chapters, and policy reports; and authored or edited 10 books, including *Multi-National Colleges and Universities: Leadership and Administration of International Branch Campuses* (2011, with Kevin Kinser), *Colleges and Universities as Economic Drivers* (2012, with Bruce Johnstone), *Academic Leadership and Governance of Higher Education* (2013, with Robert Hendrickson, James Harris, and Rick Dorman), and *Building a Smarter University* (2014). He has served on the boards of the Comparative and International Education Society (CIES), Council for International Higher Education (CIHE), the Gulf Comparative Education Society (GCES), and SUNY Korea.

DAVID LEONHARDT runs The Upshot, a *New York Times* website dedicated to covering politics and policy. The site, launched in the spring of 2014, takes a conversational, analytical approach to many of the day's biggest news stories. The Upshot also emphasizes data visualization and interactive from the *Times*'s award-winning graphics staff. Before being named to oversee the new venture in late 2013, Mr. Leonhardt was the paper's Washington bureau chief, overseeing coverage of politics, national security, the law, economics, and domestic policy from Washington. Previously, Mr. Leonhardt wrote "Economic Scene," a weekly economics column, for the business section, looking at both the broad American economy and the economics of everyday life. In April 2011, Mr. Leonhardt won the Pulitzer Prize for commentary for his columns.

BECKY KANIS MARGIOTTA (@beckykanis) is a pot stirrer, funtrepreneur, and possibility seer. Becky and her friend Joe McCannon co-founded the Billions Institute to answer one question: How do we unleash a billion people to solve the world's biggest problems in the next 50 years? As the commander of training for the institute, Becky is responsible for building a force of change agents who will transform the planet. Previously, Becky led the highly successful 100,000 Homes Campaign for Community Solutions. Featured on *60 Minutes*, the campaign was a nationwide, large-scale change effort to find and house 100,000 of the most long-term and medically vulnerable homeless people in America by July 2014. The campaign met its objective one month early. Before that, she commanded two Special Operations/Airborne companies in the U.S. Army. Becky is a graduate of the United States Military Academy and holds a master's degree from The New School. In 2013, she was recognized as a White House Champion of Change for her service to the nation as a female veteran.

JOE MCCANNON leads the Billions Institute with his friend Becky Kanis Margiotta. Joe was previously a political appointee in the Obama administration, serving as senior advisor to the administrator at the Centers for Medicare and Medicaid Services in the U.S. Department of Health and Human Services and rolling out major pieces of the Affordable Care Act. Before this, he was vice president and faculty on large-scale improvement at the Institute for Healthcare Improvement, leading the organization's major domestic initiative to improve patient safety, the 100,000 Lives Campaign, and starting its work in Africa. He has supported large-scale transformation in several nations—including Canada, Denmark, England, Japan, and South Africa—and consulted on the topic for a number of organizations, including the Bill and Melinda Gates Foundation and Community Solutions (100,000 Homes Campaign). He started his career in the publishing industry with roles at *Fast Company*, *The Atlantic Monthly*, and *Outside* magazine. He is a graduate of Harvard University and was a Reuters fellow at Stanford University.

TAYA L. OWENS currently serves the State University of New York system office of academic affairs with system-wide program implementation and research. Taya's research addresses higher education system and organizational diversity, socioeconomic development, public education policy, and educational accountability at the state and international levels. Her approach to research is founded in academics, teaching and learning, and emphasizes comparative state-level and international analysis.

JULIETTE PRICE serves as the interim director for The Albany Promise partnership. She most recently served as the education policy manager for SUNY chancellor Nancy L. Zimpher, managing various aspects of the education pipeline and multiple initiatives related to cradle-to-career partnerships, teacher education, and statewide education policy, focusing on using evidence-based interventions to improve the lives of students and families across the state of New York.

CHRISTOPHER RASMUSSEN is vice president for programs and research at the Association of Governing Boards of Universities and Colleges (AGB), where he leads the development and delivery of a comprehensive program of educational, professional development, and networking opportunities for trustees, presidents, and senior administrators in higher education. Chris joined AGB in April 2015 after nearly 10 years with the Midwestern Higher Education Compact as director and then vice president for research and policy analysis. He is a member of the Board of Trustees of Gustavus Adolphus College and an elected councilmember and mayor pro tem in Berwyn Heights, Maryland. Chris earned his PhD from the University of Michigan in public policy and higher education and a master's degree from Minnesota State University, Mankato. His professional career has included stops at Indiana University of Pennsylvania, Valparaiso University, the State Higher Education Executive Officers Association, and the University of Melbourne in Australia.

VIRAJITA SINGH is assistant vice provost in the Office of Equity and Diversity at the University of Minnesota, where she brings her expertise in design thinking, public interest design, and partnership studies to catalyze and support equity and diversity work of colleges and academic units across the university. She is also a senior research fellow and adjunct assistant professor in the College of Design, where she leads the Design for Community Resilience program she founded at the Center for Sustainable Building Research, which provides sustainable design assistance to greater Minnesota communities. From 2011 to 2015 she began and led Design Thinking @ College of Design at the University of Minnesota, a collaborative group that unleashes the creative potential of individuals and organizations across sectors to innovate in fulfilling their mission using the emerging field of design thinking. Her current academic work is focused on exploring the intersections of cultural transformation theory, partnership models, and design thinking as a strategy particularly as it applies to higher education contexts.

DAVID J. WEERTS is associate professor and faculty director of the Jandris Center for Innovative Higher Education (jCENTER) in the Department of Organizational Leadership, Policy, and Development at the University of Minnesota–Twin Cities. His scholarship and teaching focus on intersections among state financing of higher education, university-community engagement, and alumni giving and volunteerism. His research on these topics appears in a variety of scholarly venues, including *The Journal of Higher Education, Research in Higher Education, Review of Higher Education, Change Magazine,* and *Higher Education: Handbook of Theory and Research.* Professor Weerts holds a PhD in educational leadership and policy analysis from the University of Wisconsin–Madison.

NANCY L. ZIMPHER became the 12th chancellor of the State University of New York, the nation's largest comprehensive system of higher education, in June 2009. A nationally recognized leader in education, Chancellor Zimpher spearheaded and launched a new strategic plan for SUNY in her first year as chancellor. The central goal of the plan, called *The Power of SUNY,* is to harness the university's potential to drive economic revitalization and create a better future for every community across New York State. Chancellor Zimpher is active in numerous state and national education organizations and is a leader in the areas of teacher preparation, urban education, and university-community engagement. As co-founder of Strive, a community-based cradle-to-career collaborative, Chancellor Zimpher has been instrumental in creating a national network of innovative systemic partnerships that holistically address challenges across the education pipeline. She has authored or co-authored numerous books, monographs, and academic journal articles on teacher education, urban education, academic leadership, and school-university partnerships. Chancellor Zimpher currently serves as chair of the Board of Governors of the New York Academy of Sciences and of CEOs for Cities. From 2005 to 2011, she chaired the national Coalition of Urban Serving Universities. She also recently co-chaired NCATE's blue-ribbon panel on transforming teacher preparation. She previously served as president of the University of Cincinnati, chancellor of the University of Wisconsin–Milwaukee, and executive dean of the Professional Colleges and dean of the College of Education at the

Ohio State University. She holds a bachelor's degree in English education and speech, a master's degree in English literature, and a PhD in teacher education and higher education administration, all from the Ohio State University.

INDEX

benefits of college completion,
16–17, 63, 165–66; and career
readiness, 8, 129–30; and
challenges in governance, 126;
and collaborative goals, 6; and
collective impact approach, 4–6,
7, 9–13, 16–23, xi; and college
completion, 129, 172, 174, 191;
and College Scorecard, 172–73;
and colleges of education, 191–
92; competitive nature of, 8,
9–10, 19, 162; and Completion
Agenda's effort to improve
graduation rates, 19–21; and
conditions for completing a
college degree, 1–2, 11–12; and
connections with other sectors
of society, 61–62, 130; and
connection to K–12 system,
144; and connection with
Albany Promise, 158; costs
of, 61–62, 125; and course
design and faculty development,
81; and Critical Issues in
Higher Education conference
at SUNY, 5–6, 172–74, x;
cross-sector involvement
in, 131; and customized
solutions for institutions,
63, 83; and data analytics,
22, 75–76, 86; decentralized
structure of, 19, 72–73; and
demand for graduates with
degrees in science, technology,
engineering and math, 80; and
demographics, 71, 76, 85; and
design thinking, 124–26; and
difficulty with change, 9–12, 82,
85; and economic development,
8, 9, 16, 17; and economies
of scale through collective
action, 63; and educational

attainment between 1940
and 2013, 71 fig. 3.1; and
education pipeline, 2, 3, 22; and
emergence of systems, 70, 72;
and engagement in social sector,
3, 7–8, 16, 62; and enrollment
improvement, 120; and equity
gaps, 61, 63, 64, 75, 84, 85,
126; and expanding access and
completion, 7–8, 11–12, 17,
61–64, 70–72, 85, 104, 121,
125; external pressures on, 61,
62, 74; and faculty and research
considerations, 73–74, 191;
and falling in global education
rankings, 71–72; and focus
on completion, 76, 82, 84–86;
and funding on the basis of
initial enrollment, 174; and GI
Bill, 70; and Higher Education
Redesign Initiative, 125–36;
and high-impact practices, 22,
81–82; and improving student
outcomes, 61–64, 72, 76, 84,
121; and inaccessibility of in the
1940s, 70; and innovation, 133,
175; and interaction of colleges
and universities with each other
and with other sectors, 19–20,
82–84, 120–21; and isolated
impact at individual institutions,
7, 8, 21–22; and isolation, 1, 4,
7, 8, 10, 12, 23, 85; and links
with P-12 in Cincinnati, 104;
lowering costs of, 7; and math
teachers, 191–92; and mentors,
130; and multiple stakeholders,
8–9, 22, 75; and need for
transformation, 61–63, 73–74,
76, 84; and neighborhood
presence of institutions, 129;
and networks for career success,

foundations, 134; and *Grade 99* prototype, 129–32; and group work, 134–35; and investors, 128; and leaders, 131, 134; lessons learned from, 121, 125, 129, 130–33, 135–36; and model built on National Center for Public Policy in Higher Education's program, 126; and models of educational delivery, 5, 121, 125; and "Open Ticket" prototype, 129; and pilot program, 126–34; problems considered by, 127, 128; process and product objectives of, 127, 128, 130–31; and prototypes as models, 130, 131; and resulting prototypes, 128, 129–30; and selection of design associates, 126–27; and support of prototype by MN legislator, 130; and technology, 130, 131; and user fees, 134; and wide range of stakeholders, 127

High-impact Practices: and developing plans to scale up, 81; funding for, 81, 82; and learning communities, 81; and service learning, 81; and summer programs, 81; and undergraduate research, 81

high school: and Albany, NY, 147, 148, 149; and black and Hispanic students' under preparedness for college, 77; and career readiness, 152; and college readiness, 77, 106–7, 148, 149, 152; and education pipeline, 2; and graduation rates, 3, 4, 14, 74, 120; improvement in graduation rates from, 8, 14, 15, 104, 120; and

obstacles to college, 110; and Strive Partnership, 8, 14

Howard, Danette: and Critical Issues in Higher Education conference at SUNY, 5, 167, 174–76, 189–90; and importance of college degrees, 189–90; and Lumina Foundation, 167; and use of data, 181–82

innovation: and collaboration, 83–84; and committed leadership, 65, 87; conditions for failure of, 66; continuous advancement as necessary for, 64, 66; and creation of a new standard, 64; cyclical nature of, 64–66; definitions of, 64, 73; and Department of Education's Investing in Innovation Fund, 173; and design process involving stakeholders, 66, 68; and development of a business model, 65; and development of community colleges, 70; in education and research, 82, ix; and growth management, 65; and higher education shifting to a completion agenda, 84–87; and increased college completion, 63–64, 80–82; and intentional design, 79; and Jandris Center for Innovative Higher Education at University of MN, 126; and knowledge economy, 7; and learning from failure, 66; percentage of institution's budget for, 190; and problem of stagnation, 64–65; and social innovation, 10, 63–66, 68; and social mobility